Many of them also which used curious arts brought their books together, and burned them before all men; and they counted the price of them, and found it fifty thousand pieces of silver.
Acts 19:19

Monster Among Us; Curiosity

Copyright 2024

By, *William Thompson Jr*

Published By

Write Everlasting Tips
Publishing Company

Printed in the United States of America

ISBN-979-8-218-42885-3

To contact the Author write

Write Everlasting Tips Publishing Co.
P.O. Box 10854
Fort Worth, Texas 76114

Unless otherwise indicated, all scripture Quotations are from the King James Version of the Bible.

All rights reserved. Written permission must be secured from the publisher to use or reproduce any part of this book, except for brief quotations embodied in church related publications, critical review or articles.

Dedication

As an adamant advocate of Faith and Trust in the Lord Jesus Christ; Our Savior; I always make it an act of my will to speak the truth of Jesus Christ without shame or fear to all people everywhere. I know for surety, that I know who God is and that I am settled on that truthful fact! I am satisfied with God in Christ Jesus, through the power of the Holy Ghost! Ready for Jesus Christ at His return!

This work is set forth for the seeking, searching people of the earth everywhere! To those of you who think that you need to know truth at the core, from beneath the surface, I dedicate this literary work to you.

I am thankful to my family, who have always been with me, supporting me, and enduring my times of separation from them as I steal away to write what has been given for me to present to you!

Mrs. Daisy M. Thompson, Mrs. Lula M. Richard,

Mrs. Phyllis L. Jones-Thompson, Misty M. Thompson

Joseph E. Jones (Renee Jones~Taylor) Jilysia L. Jones,

Aaron L. Thompson, William Thompson III

To the Thompson and Richard Families ~ 2024

Love You All ~ *William Thompson Jr*

Table of Contents

Dedication..........................III

Introduction.....................V

1. The Danger of What If..............................21
2. Wandering Where No Mind Should Ever Wonder..49
3. Anxious Looking Too Hard To See............ 69
4. Curious of Fossils Who Put It There....................81
5. Superstitious And Skeptical........................... 91
6. Missed Them With The Truth............................105
7. Curious, But Uninterested.................................129
8. Incontinent Love...153
9. Prohibition Free Living 171

Conclusion..191

Introduction

"Monster Among Us; Curiosity"

Keep thy heart with all diligence; for out of it are the issues of life.
[Proverbs 4:23]

Monster ~ {Ugly Terrifying Being}; a large ugly terrifying animal or person found in mythology or created by the imagination, especially something fierce that kills people. Monsters often feature in folklore and fairy tales as evil beings resembling a mixture of different animals. Somebody whose perceived inhumanity or vicious behavior terrifies and disgusts people; something extraordinarily or unusually large; embryology a fetus that is markedly improperly formed, especially one that cannot live outside the uterus; an offensive term for a person, animal, or plant that is undesirably formed;

Hiding in plain sight, right in the midst of us for millenniums now, is the unrecognizable beast of disaster and destruction annihilating our faith before it can ever be released out of our belly; is the monster of the often undetectable curiosity.

We are most familiar with the Hollywood rendition of screen film monsters, of which they are, always, make believe and fake. Whatever you do, don't get it twisted, thinking that I'm referencing one of those monsters, because I'm not!

My reference is strictly given to the monstrously gargantuan spirit of uncertainty that is responsible for driving people to the left and to the right, back and forth teetering on the mid-ridge line of demarcation, between believing, exploring and total disbelief! Between trust and doubt, between acceptance and rejection; obstructing the actuality of living and walking by faith in God.

Curiosity, is the intruding audacious spirit which walk among us, right up front, in the hearts and the minds of even many who are in leadership. Who ought to be bursting forth with the spirit of God, in their leadership roles!

Being curious themselves, often they are somewhat debased and incapable of showing forth the true plan of salvation and of the power of God to do all that He says that He can and will do, through them!

I have found that curiosity causes people to feel glad about their middle of road positions, whereas they are neither accepting nor rejecting the things that would strengthen their faith in God and build a strong relationship with the Father in heaven.

They feel that they are just taking the time to examine the things which had been presented to them, a little closer. Thus leaving them in a position, to decide later on of which side to dock their own system of believing or doubting as accurate to them should those things be proven to be either true or false.

Alike many things among the churches atmosphere that is causing unrest, creating the breeding grounds for doubt and unbelief.

Not many people have been willing to fast and to pray for God to reveal this hidden blob to them which causes their focus to be foggy, and cloudy obstructing their intuitiveness to open their spirituality to see clearly. It is the stagnation of their imagination that is being described here!

So many of these people have been to the altar for prayer seeking a one shot wonder of a hand touch to rebuke the problems they experience whenever they attempt to step into faith. All along the problem is their own curiosity!

God sees your thoughts and He knows when in fact you're not really thinking of Him or His word. But what is more detrimental is the fact that He knows that you have no plans on denying your curiosity!

Deep down on the inside of you, the feeling is there that God just may in fact be incorrect about you and what it is that you're desiring to be; to have; and or even to do.

Some so-called major television ministers have taken upon themselves to announce out loud that things that they have read in the word of God are incorrect; when the bible clearly states to us that the word of God is infallible!

Often the people are allowed a variance to continue on behaving in the unfruitful manner of their previous lifestyles. Citing, that it just may be constitutionally epic for them to better research the lawful mandates of the church according to the written script of the bible, before settling in to such a change?

The problem with that kind of advice is that there is first of all no error in the word of God! The error is in the curious manner of which mere men choose to approach the written word of God. Too often, God; is not viewed as the all omnipotent, infallible God of Love, that He truly is!

It seems to me that most people are okay with

asking the questions; what's the problem; what's wrong; why can't we go further in God?

Often as if they are suggesting that God just may be the one causing the unrest and the confusion among the people of the churches? Denying them the access of faith to receive the benefits of believing God.

But, wouldn't that make God to be some kind of a schizophrenic twisted being; playing the puppet master in the sky? Be advised; that is not at all the God of the bible of which we serve in Christ Jesus; our Lord.

Although we now live in educated societies, thriving communities, not everyone applies the benefit of learning and being educated to advance the lifestyle of living and understanding life and the God given gift of living on the earth.

Many people choose to live in question as a method of neutralization against accountability and faith! Feeling that if they never acknowledge knowing, they can't be held accountable!

Of the greater citing of the courts and judicial systems, is that ignorance of the law is no excuse! Should you break the law or disregard the law, you will be held accountable with penalties; giving you the ability to know that law from now on.

So it is with the Lord according to the written word of God! God's grace and His undeniable mercy, we are often given another opportunity to

correct the error of our ways, to align our lives to reflect the mandated word of God; or maybe not?

Unlike Adam and Eve; who made a choice based on their curiosity and Satan; they were forever put out of the Garden of Eden, never having a second chance to obey or to disobey God's commandment! We are often given another chance for seeing things God's way, and given the time to correct our errors.

Whereas, we can change the direction and the manner in which we are living to please the Lord with obedience and total adherence to His word and His will for our lives.

Too many of the people of the churches are vulnerable to the satanic onslaught against the church for the simple reason that they are often yet standing in the shallow pools of curiosity!

So many who were at one time the new converts to Christ; are yet stuck right where they were whenever they first came into the church and salvation at the beginning. They have not allowed themselves to grow and to expand according to faith in God.

Alike Eve; Satan knows whenever you are curious about certain things because he's the undercover culprit responsible for encouraging the curiosity! Refusing to allow you to trust in the established ordinances of God, according to His written word.

Curiosity is often the breeding grounds for stubbornness and rebellion, for which many people have become extremely rebellious to their parents, the leadership in the churches; and eventually to their spouses.

Only, they miss the fact that "rebellion ~ begets ~ rebellion." In other words, it is not possible for you to raise obedient children when you have always been rebellious yourself!

This generation of young people; are as rebellious as they can be because they have been encouraged not to believe just because they have been taught and instructed. Instead, question everything and never to accept or receive any given knowledge or information at the first time of hearing the information.

More-so than ever; I have come into contact with people who are no longer trusting in faith in God. They feel that they have an edge on most of the people of the churches who confess to being faith believers?

They adamantly proclaim that they now question everything; they don't just believe anything! However, these same people will often take hold of the latest rumors and gossip about certain people of the churches and political arenas. Basing very judgmental decisions against them as a result without any questions.

Curiosity puts an immediate floor right beneath

you which can never even be considered to be a platform or a plateau for sustenance. Just right beneath your feet! There are no depths to be explored to that of which you are supposedly based and balanced?

In light of the fact that there is no question about what you have believed concerning Christ; curiosity comes along and suggest to you that there just might be another side to the issue? Or, erroneously, it may suggest that there is absolutely no concrete substance to the matter at hand?

In depth we are going to uncover and reveal to many, the undercover working of the spirit of curiosity which is sent to challenge every individual's grasp on the written word of God, among the faithful communities of believers worldwide!

The time has come, long since before now for us to question the questions, and to set our feet right there where we believe, and vow within ourselves never to be moved from believing and trusting the word of God.

> Curiosity ~ eagerness to know about something or to get information; eagerness or tendency to pry; an excessive interest in other people's affairs; an interesting and unusual object, person, or phenomenon..................

It is not that people have always wanted to know God; in as much as it has become their drive to know about God! What it is that makes God; to be the God; that He is indeed? From where did He originate? Where is He now?

1. Why, won't He allow me to live as I please; it's my life?
2. What Gender is God? (Male or Female)
3. Does it really matter what gender I am?
4. Is it God's business what I do with my body?
5. Is it God's business what I choose to do with your body?

It is my intention to answer many of the questions here, if not all of them! I am aware of the fact that some people will never have their questions answered, as a result of the fact that they have become questionable individuals themselves. Refusing to believe anything, they are curious about everything!

Even of the things that once made since to them, as of late they have found reason within their process of thought and of thinking, to go back and to research the matters all over again.

You're too easily accessible if someone can approach you and on their ability to paint another scenario of the things that you have believed in the written word of God for all of your life. If they can draw questions in your mind and spirit where there had never been any questions before, because you had already believed by faith?

In such situations you have failed your faith and

have turned back on God from when you first believed. It is dangerous to allow curiosity to rest in your spirit and your mind, setting up resistance to all of the knowledge and informational data, which comes your way.

Curiosity doesn't make you smarter and swifter to process data input in your own thinking capacity. It does however make you less pliable and equivalent to an accessible dumping ground!

Whereas, you are not going to be as quick to rightfully divide the word of God and to judge right from wrong! You may feel that everything, and all data, deserves an opportunity for mental examination and further scrutiny and evaluation.

The longer you allow dysgenic things to remain in your mind, they begin to erode the ability of the intellect to reasonably decipher the origin of the information and the actual direction that it may be initially designated to lead you.

Curiosity creates conjecture and it seriously offends the cause of faith and can turn belief into unbelief. Thus canceling every opportunity to know God in the fullness of His spirit and power.

This is the ultimate reason that most people in the churches have not received the infilling of the Holy Ghost; with the evidence of speaking in tongues; to eventually manifest the fruit of the spirit!

Healing and miracles, of all sorts, cannot be seen

in the churches, as a result of the assassination to the desired faithful adherence in people, all because of their curiosity.

Curiosity paints and alternative picture of all the things that are of God and of the churches. Suggesting the possibility to the people, of another form of worship? Even as suggest by Opra Winfrey; there just may be many paths to God?

Never encouraging them to embrace the only truth that Jesus Christ; is the only path to God. As written and stated in the word of God!

It is definitely erroneous thinking to believe that curiosity will let you into faith, or into the depths in the word of God! Or finally, that it will let you into the mind of God whereas you can know the things that are unavailable to merely the human psyche.

The scripture states that He; God in Christ Jesus; is able to do exceeding abundantly; above all that we can ask or think! [Ephesians 3:20] paraphrasing by the author.

Whenever we trust in the truth of God, we discover even the more, just how much there is to know that we will never know! For as long as we are living in the flesh, on this earth!

Were it not for the spirit of curiosity, people would not have been so bent on redefining their normality, and or so determined to explore an alternative side of their own true physicality.

People are infuriated in their spirits, along the linage of racial relations, and burned in their own lust as it relates to sexual origins, and sexual agendas, genders, orientations and preferences.

I would like to think that one of the greater purposes for giving gifts at birthdays and Christmas; for weddings and graduations exercises, is for the benefit of teaching us to receive and to accept that to which we have been given with gratitude and with the gratefulness of heart.

I am coming to the greater understanding that people are not nearly so much as ungrateful as they are often curiously wondering in their minds of the things that they did not get, or receive.

Too often people are thinking that what they want is far better that what they have been given. Jesus; is standing before the scribes and the Pharisees teaching and giving a parable to them; but they responded to Him saying; give us a sign, show us of things to come.

He was giving them the words of eternal life; but they wanted a show of His ability, according to His own confession. He referred to them as a perverse generation; a stiff necked generation. He warned them that there would be no sign given to them but as of that of the prophet Jonah;

As Jonah was in the belly of the fish for three days and three nights; so shall the son of God be in the heart of the earth for three days and for three nights. He says to them you seek a sign, yet a greater than Jonah is here! [Matthew 12:] paraphrasing..................

The people of these present generation's scientific and political arenas, are talking about life and living on the planet Mars. As if that is really at all possible. We have all been given the gift and the benefit of living on the earth, yet they feel that they just might do better on another planet?

Maybe God would not be there?

Where they could come up with such thinking is certainly beyond any curiosity of my own mind! As a matter of the fact, I would never want to even think of being anywhere else but in Heaven! If I am not going to be here on the earth any longer.

They are in discussion of taking the non-returnable trip to Mars; whereas if they find that living there is totally impossible, they're finished and doomed forever, never being able to return to earth.

What it is that they are attempting to escape is only imaginary; as there is absolutely no escape from God of the Universe!

Who is responsible for anyone thinking that the possibility of living anywhere else is even possible?

Perhaps they need to understanding the fact that they/we were all born on the face of this planet; earth, by God's divine design!

Should there have been another place for living I'm sure that God would have made it available to all of mankind to have been born there also!

The question is; Is it really possible to get away from life and living as we know of it and have known of it to this present day? [Genesis 1:]

Although they have not at all successfully mastered living harmoniously, here on the earth with the people God created for us all to live with. They wonder if living on Mars will give to them the separation they have desired for centuries now.

It is devastating that people believe in separation while they curiously ponder being lost in the crowd, should they come together as a people of the one humanistic society.

Even many leaders have been too curious seeking ways into the finances of the people, rather than to lead the people straight down the path into the word of God; instead!

They should be more interested to the entry into the heart and the minds of the people. Teaching them the ways of the spirit of God. Teaching them to know Him in the fullness of His power.

Showing the people how to be open to having a right relationship with God. The issue of curiosity is such the monstrosity of a reality; having been in existence since from the beginning of time. Satan have always desired to stand in the way between man and of faith, and the truth our

God.

While he has not been totally successful at keeping us from faith in God, he has been detrimental to our faith through the curiosity of our minds.

He has been successful at keeping the people of the churches looking away, often denying them the ability to be focused and to stay focused on our God.

People focus on a lot of things, but not many are able to say that they are truly focused on the Lord. They see a lot of things, and hear a lot of stuff, but most of the things which come our way are often only distractions to our faith.

Can you see how we have been curiously distracted in our walk with the Lord?

The greater problem lies within the fact that there are so many people equally as curious which lends to the ungodly society's acceptance and support to their disbelief.

Whenever we feel that there are so many other people being plagued with the same type of struggles or attacks upon their faith, even though they have never surrendered their faith to the Lord;

Likewise, as of the faith of those of us who are frequently in the church, we tend to feel the need to be supportive of their plight since we have never found the solutions to the problems either?

We dropped the ball, as a faith filled supporter never getting to the bottom of the issue, or refusing to believe that curiosity is the foundational, root of the problem.

It rests upon the fact that curiosity has been sent to assassinate our faith in God!

People are always sure that everything is not alright; they know there's a problem with them, and they know that they don't have what it takes to fix the brokenness; however they are not open to the finding of the fact that the problem lies within the curiosity of their own mind.

Stabilize the curiosity of your minds, and take control of your ability to accept the truth, as it is!

One

"Dangers; Of What If~?"

For what if some did not believe? Shall their unbelief make the faith of God without effect? God forbid: yea, let God be true, but every man a liar; as it is written, that thou mightest be justified in thy sayings, and mightest overcome when thou art judged. [Romans 3:3-4]

"Always in Question"

The sensitivity of this topic demands that I approach this chapter of discussion, somewhat delicately. As people are very sensitive and quite touchy as it relates to being scrutinized closely to reveal the truth about their chosen decisions of belief.

I make no concession to you that I will avoid touching that sore place of curiosity that may indeed lie deeply within you. Which may have taken hold of you to become the supervising companion, speaking in you louder than the internal call for you to make a decision.

It is not only that the monstrous oppositional struggle with curiosity, which rest so greatly within the heart of the people in our purported atmospheres of believers nowadays;

It is though, however; that many of the same people who are active members of the local congregations of Christ centered churches, that have chosen to be seated right up front in the midst of all whom are questioning God's reality and the truth of the word of God!

They are ignorantly denying themselves the faith ascribed by the scripture. They seek a more acceptable explanation of faith which just may exclude God, and the written word of God; altogether! Which is the only authority of acquiring the faith that supplies all of God's benefits, associated to being faithful.

No matter what the scripture says about having faith and trusting in the Lord; they think that they just might not be wrong, haven chosen the position to question faith, all together?

> How shall they call of him in whom they have not believed? And how shall they believe in him of whom they have not heard? And how shall they hear without a preacher? And how shall they preach except they be sent? As it is written, how beautiful are the feet of them that preach the gospel of peace, and

> BRING GOOD TIDINGS OF GOOD THINGS. BUT THEY HAVE NOT ALL OBEYED THE GOSPEL. FOR ESAIAS SAITH, LORD, WHO HATH BELIEVED OUR REPORT? SO THEN FAITH COMETH BY HEARING, AND HEARING BY THE WORD OF GOD.
> ROMANS 10:14-15

Such environments are not only conducive for sinful lifestyles, they also create more comfortable platforms for psycho-analytical stages of thinking, for those who choose to live contrary to the word of the scripture.

The curiosity which lies so deeply within people, whereas they have chosen to upstage their own reasonable theology of God, have got them questioning whether God could have possibly ever meant what He said in the bible or not? Or, did He even say those things that are written in the scripture?

Curiosity is going to alleviate the ability to know what God is indeed saying to this generation through His written word. People willfully allow for themselves to be denied the reality and the truth of God's word, as it has been written, already.

Receiving Jesus Christ; as Lord and savior has been taught, although ignorantly erroneous? The bible scriptures have been taught controversially, to suggest contradiction between the Old Testament and the New Testament. Even though Jesus Christ; clearly states that He did not come to condemn the law, but to fulfill the law.

More frequently, the preferred biblical approach of the scripture is to question rather than to believe and to receive the only infallible written word of God.

Willfully, many people have given themselves to think along the lines of the things they might do that they know are in-

deed sinful and wrong, thinking; what if the bible is wrong?

More people are postured to fight against the mandate of the scripture, struggling against the need to be governed and led by the word of God in their decisions and their lifestyles.

Daily we see this played out in the social media when certain court cases are aired publicly. They argue along the lines of people having the rights to choose on many diverse political platforms, and sociable issues;~ i.e. abortion rights; gender alterations; same-sex marriages; What the people of the churches have the right to do or not; and on and on……….

As these wars are aired out to the public, people tend to believe that God in some way or another, might have lost His position in the hearts of the people; and in reality at large?

This generation now considered itself smarter in these latter times, since the days of the people back in the bible days? However, as more information is made available, the educated acquisition of knowledge will have no diminishing power against the reality of God! God Is!

Unintelligently; people have backed away from personally being acquainted with God! Their choices are for nothing more than applying the world's methods and contemptible schemes of influence to acquire more stuff and to live more comfortably.

People now have more, even though they refuse to believe and to trust in God as their provider. That doesn't give credence to deny faith in God. Lots of people only want a bunch of stuff and material possessions, they don't want God!

They are not intending to bring recognition to the things that God is doing on a consistent basis, that really does be-

speak of His goodness to us. They feel that to brandish their stuff and their material possessions establishes the only reasonable right to say that God is indeed good.

Sort of aids in the spiritual blindness of the unbelieving outsiders of faith in God; to hear the people of the churches say that God is good?

People are now falling away from seeking God to supply their need because they never trust that God has no respect of persons, even though the bible says that God have no respect of persons! [Acts 10:34]

They had not been awarded the exact same financial favor ability of being able to acquire all of the desired stuff, as some other people that they might have come into contact with. They have become embittered disbelieving in the integrity of the Lord, to care for them.

So those on the outside that are curious about God; always in question about the operation of the spirit of God; and all of the things that pertain to God; as they decide that they are going to seek God for themselves; they collide with people in the churches projecting this same carnal demeanor of distrusting God, failing to believe in Him.

They in the churches, that have got lots of stuff, they may be favored with better opportunities than those that don't have much. It is not often favorable for them that may be on the lower end, while struggling their way, learning to have faith in God? They are not as strong as they will be relative to receiving and knowing God; in the pardoning of their sins.

Many others, not willing to stand the testing of having faith in God, will often choose to remain in sin because they already have lots of stuff and the finer things that money can buy. So, why do I need God; is what they may think and are not afraid to speak out of their mouths?

The people of the churches are responsible for causing many people to doubt God; when it is our responsibility to cause men to believe God; without a doubt! God has done so much more for all of us that have nothing at all to do with money!

There is no way to believe and to doubt simultaneously; thinking with the very same mind. But, while they are indeed curious, they are also a bit confused and unsure about the people of the churches.

You Might Have Been Taught To Doubt, But Be Sure Instead.

Either you are going to believe or you are going to doubt, refusing to believe. As a boy coming up in the 60s-70s-80s; many of the adults of our community had a saying in response to many of the questions that we would ask of them. As a way of putting us off, but preventing us from feeling that they were ignoring us, they would say; "I doubt it!"

Not realizing what they were indeed doing to most of us. They were actually teaching us doubtfully, to exist in the middle of the road. Refusing to choose a direction to travel concerning truth and the many questions that would come our way.

I keep saying that our words are powerful and they often have binding effects in the minds of the people that we come into contact with. Most people, are prone to never forget what you have said to them, especially whenever it wasn't the truth.

So many people are now plagued with the spirit of indecisiveness. Resulting from dealing with people who would never take a stand and say which side they were indeed standing on, without a doubt.

We'd like to believe that people are in denial about most things, being the defining reasons that they don't move forward in life? However, the greater truth is that they refuse to make definite choices that would put them on a determined path.

I must inform you that people are more-so living in total refusal to make the decision to move either backwards or forwards; to the left or to the right; or to stay centered steadfastly focused on God!

They doubt the benefits of either decision, so in refusal, often without even knowing it, they have bought into the idea that they just might have forever to make a decision? Even though they are getting older by the minute, the hour, and by the day!

My friend; we do not have forever to make the right decision to get things right with our lives, our families, our souls and to be in right standings with God like the bible says it!

It is sad to me that so many people feel that they are actually living more freely as result of thinking and believing that they are staying in the middle. They are always in question, but forever refusing to hear an answer to the questions that they have.

People are posturing themselves as if to suggest that they are indeed better off being open to the ideas of there being possible non-truths written in the bible? The people of the churches who are curious about believing all that is written in

the bible, they just might also be deceived about God's word?

Educators are now in a bigger hurry to inflate the egos and the minds of the children. Teaching them to scientifically evaluate and to question everything and never to believe what they see, hear, and or even what they are witness to.

As it relates to the miracle working power of God, whereas they are witnesses, it is suggested to them that it is better to believe that it had all been a trick! They shouldn't to believe what they had just witnessed.

Yet they are taken to the magic shows and to the circus to witness the tricks and the magicians, and encouraged to take up with the ability to do magic tricks and to hold hostage the imaginations of the people.

The society believes that it is better to have people in question than to have them disappointed when being denied access to the real power of God; because of their unbelief.

One thing is for sure, people do whatever they feel they are big enough and grown enough to do, and they don't want anyone or anything telling them what they cannot do! Believing in the "Lord Jesus Christ;" means surrendering to Him; with our total being, denying ourselves.

Lots of people are in their graves today because they would never make a decision to either hear from someone who could have helped them to escape their destiny with death too soon! Or, to move themselves to be properly positioned to be passed over by the untimely collision with death through their faith in God's almighty power!

A simple decision can often be lifesaving as well as it can also be life changing. Life; itself is uncertain, we don't know what will befall us from moment to moment; anything that can happen is subject to happen right out of the blue!

We use to say; "here today, and gone tomorrow!" Now the reality is that we're here today and gone today! Right now is no guarantee of any future existence of later on, after a while; or on another day. People lay down at night having plans for tomorrow, curious about how things will turn out for their plans, only to never be allowed to see the next day as planned?

They are so curious, they fail to realize that tomorrow has never been promised to them. They are unable to fathom the devastation they will experience when things go wrong!

It can be overwhelming to finally realize that the problem all along has been your refusal to allow yourself to develop into the matured decision making individual. But in the right now reality of the need for you to make proper decisions for your life. That is a requirement for living by assured faith in today's world.

You may have been blaming everyone else for the disastrous wrecks of your life, based on feeling that somebody should do those kinds of things for you. You may feel that you're not good at making decisions and choosing because of the questions you have about everything?

As people are often desiring to know God; their approach is launched from the very same standpoint that every other decision is made in their lives. They are looking at *THIS*', but they are equally curious about *THAT*', at the very same time!

Curiously wondering, they settle on the idea that God; can be explored through dissecting his word, without applying faith to trust the truth of His word? Rather, than faithfully

believing; just in case things don't work out between them and God they may seek to remain neutral?

It's a reality that so many people appear to be stuck back at the beginning of their experience with God! This is the reason in fact that so many people are feeling that they actually need more from the church! They feel that they need to hear so much more than just the gospel of Jesus; they think anyway?

Most of the people who have listened to the gospel as it might have been preached in a sermon from the pulpit; they have never really heard it! The truth of the gospel never reached their hearts!

Many of the leaders have fallen prey to the schemes of hustling the people for their money; curious about the possibilities of bringing more people in to the fellowship of their churches. Which will inevitability amass a much greater financial base.

As a result, many of them are stuck on stupid right there, disregarding the admonishment of the scripture. Jesus teaches us; that we cannot serve both mammon and God. [St. Matthew 6:24]

Jesus knows that curious people will never see God; alone of themselves. They will be blinded by their own minds obscuring the visibility of seeing in the spirit, covered by the lust of their flesh; the lust of their eyes and the pride of life. [I John 2:16]

It used be normal back in the latter years for the smaller ministries to be the more successful churches, as it related to the people being led to have more real relationships with the Father in Heaven.

As of late, even the smaller churches have been plagued with the curiosity of desiring what it might feel like to have more people in their ministries, than they have presently?

They have become somewhat like the man who was giving the one talent, but in reverse. Though they were yet in fear, they didn't bury the talent. Rather, they put their talent out there to be manipulated to produce growth, but all for the wrong reasons! Yet because of fear!

The man given the one talent was afraid that something would happen to the talent if he did not hide it and put it away to safe keeping? However, these leaders are afraid that nothing will happen for them unless they put forth their talent to manipulate, to make something happen, feeling they need to help God! Because the people are not coming in to their churches as they would like to see!

Curious leaders doubt that God is going to prosper the church, so they think within themselves that they need desperately to make some things happen for themselves, else their churches will die?

Not realizing that having that kind of stinking thinking in their heads and in their hearts, that their churches are already dead.

>EXCEPT THE LORD BUILD THE HOUSE, THEY LABOR IN VAIN THAT BUILD IT: EXCEPT THE LORD KEEP THE CITY, THE WATCHMAN WAKETH BUT IN VAIN.   [PSALMS 127:1]

What If Praying And Prayer Won't/Will Do It

Many people will go ahead at times and pray for the purpose of seeking the Lord for help. But they had not been taught that starting their prayer with "IF", truthfully assassinates any faithful connectivity to the Father in Heaven to fulfill their need!

The greater problem is that they don't know the word of God. [Hebrews 11:6]

Listening to the wrong people's description of prayer, they think that it's in the proper order to fleece God, thinking that they are putting God to the test, as if even they are doing God a favor by even coming to Him; in the first place?

My friend; your prayer is canceled from the beginning, the very moment that you allow the word "if" to inundate the dialogue from your mouth. You are saying to the Lord; that you have not believed anything about asking God to do anything for you in prayer.

Of course; in the past I have heard people say with my own ears, that they prayed; "Lord if you are what they say you are then do this for me; and God did it! But they also came back to say well ("I guess that He is") what they say that He is?

They never confessed to being totally convinced that God is God; and they never committed to changing their lifestyles to live for God! Being intelligent enough to utter some words on your knees does not suggest that you are entering into a faithful prayer dialogue with the Lord!

Your willingness to doubt the Lord disallows the needed connection between yourself and the Lord. Prayer is not just you saying a bunch of words to the Lord, but it's about allowing the Lord to speak with you in response to what you have asked of Him.

> BECAUSE THAT, WHEN THEY KNEW GOD, THEY GLORIFIED HIM NOT AS GOD, NEITHER WERE THANKFUL; BUT BECAME VAIN IN THEIR IMAGINATIONS, AND THEIR FOOLISH HEART WAS DARK-

When they recognized that it was God who did it for them, they weren't thankful to God to the point in fact that they would acknowledge Him from now on.

Curiosity breeds shame and embarrassment; God has done so much for so many people who are too ashamed to acknowledge it in the presence of their own doubting society of friends and family members. They will not even testify of His true goodness and reality.

Many of those same people feel that just because they happened to collide with the mercy of God; they will be awarded to live eternally with Him, as if it is their reward for allowing Him to intervene in their life?

See one of the greatest dangers of "what if"; is that it will leave you on the outside of where it is that you desire to be and even of where you ought to be, as it relates to communicating with God.

Only; in most cases, you're the only person who doesn't know that you have failed to make the connection! Whenever you have made the connection with God; people everywhere that you go will know that you have been with God!

God always leaves a deposit with us signifying as a witness that we have been in His presence.

The number one goal ought to be that you are sure that you have completed the task of communicating with the Lord the moment that you went down on your knees; or wherever it may have been that you entered into a prayer dialogue.

So many people have been taught to say to the Lord; "if

you're real"? Of which, if you would study your bible you will see that is the language of Satan! [St. Matthew 4:3]

People who purport to be a witness for the Lord often meet people who refuse outright to pray or to even believe that God; really is God!

So as they prod those people pushing them to go ahead and pray to Him; in the name of Jesus. They suggest to them to check the reality and the validity of God's existence. Say to Him; "God if you're really real, hear me, or can you do this or that for me?"

The greater indictment against them is when they try and broker a deal with God, by making promises that they have no idea how they are going to be able to keep the promises they have made to Him.

Without a doubt; you understand that God keeps good records; and He remembers the vows and the promises that we make to Him.

Although the scripture informs us of the fact that God will remember our sins no more when we will have repented of our sin to Him. [Hebrews 10:17]

It is not the sins of the past that we need to be concerned with, it is the dishonored vows and the promises that we have made and have not even looked back to remember them since the moment we got up from our knees in prayer to Him.

"What If" says that just maybe God didn't take us seriously while we were on our knees? Perhaps He knows that we've changed our minds since the fear wore off or since we got what we asked for. Or that we never really meant what we said to Him?

The spirit of curiosity working on the inside of you, will immediately begin to suggest to you that you were so silly and ridiculous? To think that an invisible God, up in the sky somewhere, would care that much for you, to hear you and to answer your prayer?

I have prayed for some people who could not be healed through medicine and through the treatment of their doctors. Anointing them with oil, I laid my hands on them in the name of Jesus, and they were raised from their death beds and from their sickness, not even needing their medication anymore!

Those same people will not even give God the credit for their healing. They accredit the doctors and the medicine and the surgeries that they had gone through as being the remedy for their near death experience.

So many people that I have ministered to, who have indeed been delivered and set free, their lives have changed! Their bodies are forever healed, whereas; they have never experienced what they were going through before the Lord led me to pray for them. They looked at me with that "iffy" kind of spirit, knowing that others had chosen not to acknowledge me?

For several decades now, they are yet to even mention my name to other people, acknowledging that the Lord used me to minister to them?

Some people who refused to acknowledge me have gone back into their conditions but even further than they were before; and some of them are now sleeping in their graves. God used me; I did not go out to them on my own!

Some of those people did not just refuse to acknowledge me as the called and ordained Prophet of God that I am; they chose to put their mouths on me speaking negatively! But I'm in good company to the patriarchs of the scripture.

The danger is that whenever you approach the man and the woman of God with the spirit of what if; questioning their authenticity and their integrity; you are actually questioning the authenticity of God who called and sent them!

So many people have decided to look everywhere else to either try to find God or to erase the idea of God, and to diffuse the reality of Jesus Christ; altogether.

Other religions have based their foundational basis on that they believed that the story of Jesus Christ was fabricated and totally untrue!

Easily persuaded, people believe that the bible is total fiction! As a result, they are often found giving their time to scientific research of the bible, going back into historical documentation believing that they will find the truth? [II Timothy 6:20]

It's painful to hear people suggest that the bible is false and fiction, as I am persuaded that the word of God is true! As I can see the scriptures coming to pass day by day! The bible was here before any of us on the face of the earth today ever got here.

You may indeed be an expert at researching information; but you have not been awarded the ability to go back before the truth and reality of God; to determine whether or not He; really is who He says that "HE IS!"

People are making video documentations suggesting that the bible was created by man to control the lives of people?

They now believe that we have developed and advanced in education to the point that there is no need for the bible or even for the church now!

They are even suggesting that there should be apologies given for causing the people to fear going to hell as a result of living sinfully wicked and ungodly; which is simply their choices.

People won't read and study the bible; but they will spend hours of research on the bible trying to discredit the authenticity of the scripture.

They will go out of their way to prove that living by the bible is not necessary or important. They feel that we are now beyond that.

The world has come out of the closet in every level of sinning and of self; seeking to prove that there is no more fear of the scripture or for God! They are even verbalizing that they are going to hell and that they are proud of that decision. How deceived is that?

Since the people of most of the churches still believe that sin is still sin and that it will take you to hell; the people of the courts and the State's Legislative committees have taken it upon themselves to discredit the mandate of the scripture. They have chosen to legalize what the bible has indeed declared as sin. People are now living out loud in sin, in public display without any shame; they think anyway?

Only because they now have a larger support base for their chosen lifestyle of disobedience to the scripture; somehow they feel that they have forced the hand of God to accept them and to open the gates of Heaven to them; if Heaven is

really real?

"What if;" suggest to the secular society that the churches who are comprised of the blood-washed people of God; that we have no given authority to show them through the scriptures that their lifestyles will cause them to be in hell forever! After they will have lived sinfully and wickedly never haven repented for their sins .

Do you ever wonder why it is that so many people don't want to believe in God? Why are they so angry at the idea of surrendering their life to Him? Why is it that they are so determined to believe that Jesus Christ just can't be real; even though, other than the bible, there are historical documents that testify of the existence and the works of Christ; that He did?

Do you ever wonder why it is that people choose prayer as a last option, only if they can't make it happen on their own? I know for sure that people don't want to feel that they are obligated to give reverence to God for the things that He will have done for them.

They are loyal to all of their skeptical family and friends who also believe that the bible is an intrusion to their chosen lifestyles. So out of loyalty they choose to avoid at all cost, to pray in the name of Jesus Christ.

Many of the people who led them to disbelieve in the truth of Jesus Christ are now dead and sleeping in their graves! They have gone on to the reality of having to face the truth of God and His word in eternity. Even in death they have got a hold on the people left behind that they influenced to disbelieve.

What if you realized that your true loyalty is to someone

who have been in the grave for decades now? Did you not realize that you can believe in the one who is really alive and well forever more? Jesus Christ did die on the cross and was buried in the borrowed tomb of Joseph; but God raised Him from the grave, alive! After three days with all power in His hands; He is alive! And He lives forever more!

Their followers feel that they are betraying the teaching of their past mentors, should they acknowledge the truth that have been revealed to them, now in the absence of their mentors.

People are also very embarrassed to realize that God is who He says that He is indeed! He can do everything but fail! They are out-done that God was able to do what their educated college instructors and professors; their doctors and their lawyers could not do for them.

I would much rather live for God knowing that He is; rather than to die and find out that He is after having denied the faith and the truth of who is; for all of my life!

It is appalling to me that secular humanist have the audacity to give their own washed out definition of what the soul is and their determination of designation for the purpose the soul.

There is no individual on the face of the planet who has any authority over the souls of man. Not even Satan has the authority over the souls of mankind, else no one would ever surrender their souls to the Lord Jesus Christ; Satan would see to that!

Curiosity makes the mind sick; it opens the portals of the mind to spiritual attack and to demonic domination. There are so many things written in the scripture that God declares

to be evil.

There are levels of sinning that most people who are tender hearted towards the word and to the will of God would never knowingly explore with the determination to reach those stubborn, and rebellious levels of sinning.

Most simple minded people simply believe that what God says couldn't possibly be correct and that it is indeed wrong and not up for any discussion with them. Ungodly people open their mouths to speak against God; and they go even further to curse God; being the fools who have declared that there is no God!

There used to be a time that people were even careful how they handled the bible; now being skeptical and unbelieving they will take the bible and throw it against the wall and set fire to it. Even though there are times that it will not even burn.

More boldly than ever before now, people are comparing the Bible to the Koran; and to the Torah and other religious writings. Attempting to discredit the written scriptures of the bible.

In these times of which we are now living, people have determined to mesh Hip Hop with Christianity; thinking that God just may not know how they should express themselves in the churches and in the communities?

They are all in the churches dancing to secular music, the musicians who used to be dedicated the service of the Lord without dividing their hearts, are now determining that it's okay to play in the clubs and in the church; simultaneously!

They have made up in their own minds to use the scripture

against God! So that they can use their God given gifts and talents of playing musical instruments to make money. But, for demoniacally influenced atmospheres and very secular venues.

When they see that they have sinned and that they are acting as if they had never known the Lord, they take it upon themselves to blame God for the behavior of those people who are not living as they should either!

They even take it upon themselves to believe that if the people of the church can sin and get away with it, then they ought to be able to stay in sin and never be held accountable.

They who have determined to stay with the church just in case; in their skepticism and doubt about the things of God; they have desecrated the sanctity of the churches creating the secular club atmospheres, so as to make going to church more comfortable to those who have determined to never surrender to the Lord.

The church sanctuaries are now being rented out to anybody with the money for all sorts of secular purposes; even for that which is totally against God!

Hearing the ungodly voices from Hollywood; people are convinced that it is okay to mix with the people of the world who totally reject the reality of God.

For an instance; everything about Halloween is associative to the devil and of all that is evil. But so many of the churches are allowing parties and commemorative celebrations for this secular day of the devil.

It is to the greater detriment of the people in the churches who refuse to believe the bible's report of the devil and of how

it is that he came to be.

It is the churches responsibility to see that the fears of the people is relieved and done away with. Secular society thinks that it's healthy to be afraid and to experience great fear. We are witnesses that certain people have failed to fear when they should have; they suffered emanate death and total destruction.

What if; leaves people in utter confusion as to what it is that they are to fear and to be afraid of. Allowing them to get caught up in the wrong thing, at the wrong place, at the wrong time.

At the demise of these certain people, others are left to question "what if" they had only known; would they have still been alive right now? Only, eventually the revealed truth is that they knew the danger, but refused to believe that the danger would actually be deadly to them.

Many weather disasters are the results of those who see that the water has risen beyond its borders and has overflowed barriers and roadside edges. The false security of "what if;" I can make it? The news and their loved ones are now plagued with the report of losing them to the raging flood.

People, who see the signs of the time; know that the world is raging to an uncertain end soon! They have become so skilled at questioning everything, they refuse to pay attention to any signs of uncertainty, thinking that they just might be in control of their own fate?

Somehow people feel that all things will be solved and worked out for humanity in the Science Laboratory?

People are even led to believe that somehow humanity can

move around in the earth and avoid situational disasters of all sorts.

It is ridiculously believed that somehow, someway, that people are going to find a way to change the mind of God to the point that He will accept the way that the people of the earth are now seeing things.

I believe God and the word of God! I'm determined to show you according to the scripture that He is not at all encouraged to see things your way! In Genesis chapter 11; Nimrod led to people in building a tower to heaven? They thought to themselves, "what if" we really can make it to heaven on our own skills and our own thinking?

Whoever told them exactly where Heaven was located above the earth, and in which direction they needed to build a tower to get there? "What if," they would have made it to heaven, and what difference would it have made being that they were not heavenly beings?

They were all indeed human beings made to live in the earth, they were never created to live or to even visit heaven in their flesh. Too many people in the flesh sort of think that they are able to do in the flesh that of which can only be done in the spirit, or in the spiritual realm.

People; disbelieve in the powerful ability of faith in God; while they go out of their way to bolster what has been proven to be the inabilities of the flesh or of their natural beings.

They live with the attitude of saying; "what if" I can anyway? I have heard people say of the word of God; I know what the bible says, but, "what if" the bible missed something; and I can do this or that anyway?

It is too dangerous of a chance to take, thinking "what if" God really is not mad at sin and the devil? Some teach that well if you do go to hell, you're already dead, and you'll just burn up and that will be it! Hell is not the same as cremations!

Even though the bible clearly states that those in hell will burn forever, because mere men cannot even fathom what forever will be, as things in the earth have been given an ingrained time frame for lasting, they have decided that hell cannot last forever either.

There is no scientific experiment that will ever be able to disprove how long that eternity will last, or how long an everlasting fire can burn.

All of the horrors of hell are everlasting; all that is in hell have been there ever since hell was created; the only difference is that hell is a place once begun that can never end.

No need to be curious as to how your friends and your loved ones are doing in hell? I can help you with that question, they are not doing well at all! They are in total destruction and eternal torment forever, as they will never do well ever again.

My friends, the imagination can neither create nor recreate the reality and the truth to what already is, it has the greater ability to only suggest "what if "a particular thing could be? We must be watchful never to allow our imaginations to live in the realms of the possibility of what might be or even of what could be; if?

So many who never take advantage of the things they presently have to work with, are always seeking the paths into getting their hands on making their possibilities real.

Dangers, Of What If?

Although it doesn't exist, they are determined somehow or another to bring the impossible into the realm of the possible; to make the fictitious a now reality.

Some people; you are never going to convince them that certain things just doesn't exist. I have set up in the night with people who were tormented over a certain thing. No matter how I talked with them and even though we prayed, they would not embrace the fact that thing did not exist.

Their greater determination of thinking was that; "what if" it does exist? People don't understand how they are denigrating themselves preparing to take actions against a thing that will never come to pass, because the whole thing is false; it doesn't exist! It's not real!

People who won't do what they can do are often more determined to do what they can't do; for all sorts of reasons! Even the people, who have become somewhat skilled at robbing the banks, stores and all sorts of financial institutions, they have also failed in knowing how to get away with the crime that they have committed!

Although they prepare to escape, having the getaway driver in place; something unexpected goes wrong with the escape route. Although they didn't get away that time, they have vowed not to get caught the next time?

There is something about a wrong thing ending in a wrong way that will not always award the thinking process of the perpetrator of the vile action, to change their mind on doing wrong.

Curiosity is so strong inside of them, that it pushes them to an even greater measure to try again, sometimes at even the

very same place in the company of the very same people.

Insanely, they have determined that they will have a very different outcome, although nothing at all has been changed! They did the very same thing, and at the very same place of location, and in the very same manner that it was done previously!

People fail to know and to believe that it is ordained of God that thieves and murderers, and all who commit different acts of sin, for them to be caught and held responsible, and accountable for their actions.

Just because it might appear that everybody is doing a certain thing of sin or error, it doesn't mean that you will not be the one chosen to show everybody else that it is indeed the wrong thing to do.

People you have got to check the curiosity on the inside of you. It is more than necessary to know why it is that you are so curious; even to the point that you are seeking support of those who are probably just as curious as you are yourself.

Finding Five Million people who are being plagued with the same curiosities as you, doesn't silence the word of God concerning that area of sin which you seek desperately to explore.

God made you and formed you and put you in the earth. You did not form or create God and put Him in Heaven on the throne.

Because sin and iniquity is in the churches and in the land more vastly than ever before; the imaginations of people is driving them more wildly than has ever been witnessed since mankind has been on the earth.

People who have television platforms are now teaching things with a bible in their hands that are not at all from the Lord; even according to the bible in their hands.

It is no wonder that people are advancing in worldly matters more so than people are increasing and advancing in the Kingdom of God.

You will never get to the right intended destination while traveling the wrong direction! Some people give the success of baking a cake to the name brand mixer that is used. You can mix all of the wrong ingredients for a week; it still won't make a cake?

Others swear by their oven's make and model, but it is neither the right oven which makes the cake. It is however; obedience to the proper mixture of the right ingredients; and the proper temperature of the oven, having knowledge of the perfectly allotted time for baking, and the proper baking utensil that will guarantee successfully baking the cake.

It is far past the hour of being too late, and way too much time has been wasted while you've been trying to decide "what if"; the time is now for you to come out of that place of curiosity and believe to the point of knowing who God is; and knowing that He is!

Two

"Wandering, Where No Mind Should Ever Wonder"

"The Questions Are Carnally Curiously; The Answers are Spiritually Discerned"

I am blown away at the inflated arrogance of the influential injustice viciously levied against people around the globe, for having faith in God, through Christ Jesus our Lord and savior of the world!

Bombshell-like arguments of all types of idealisms and non-biblical methodologies for sub-standards of livings, from all genres of media through technology of the Internet, television, and yet even through public speaking platforms. Raining down atop of the mental configuration of all people who are subject to hearing, to receive all that has been purported as consenting to disregard the written truth of God's word.

So as to counteract adherence to the truth of God, from the authoritative positions of leadership in Government, Higher learning Institutions, Corporate Hirelings and of the following laymen of communities in both the religious, and the secular societies alike.

People that refuse to believe God according to the written word, through the spell driven curiosity in their own minds, go out of their own ways through metaphysics and science; to call the very truth of God into question!

As if they have the authority to demand a sense of accountability from God. They seek secular data and or information which might inform them of God's beginning and of His end! Refusing to accept the fact that "God' IS!" From everlasting to everlasting, no beginning and never an end!

Their real true purpose is to defy the actuality of the biblical account of Christ Jesus. Who being born of the spirit of God, thus being The Spirit of "God!" Yet, through obedience He became the begotten image of God, who became flesh and dwelt among us right here in the earth. To reveal the truth and power of the grace and love of God for us all. To save us from the darkened penalty of sin and death; and the eternal destruction of the second death of the soul in the lake of fire.

Questions that we think that we humanely have for God; in Christ Jesus; through the power of the Holy Ghost; have already been addressed and provided in the written scriptures of the bible. People need but to read and to study the written word of God just as diligently as they vigorously go after researching, seeking a validated reason for disbelieving the account of the scripture!

It is paramount that we individually determine within ourselves to receive what the scripture says without questions. Rather refusing to doubt, as we were not there in the presence of those who gave their own witnessed accounts! At which time all doubtful interrogations and uncertainties of the scriptures will be resolved! II Timothy 3:16

Amazingly, as it relates to the creative authority and to the power of God; people consistently allow for their minds to wonder about the speculative clouds of analysis in their heads questioning! Cumulatively collecting more questions relative to the reasons when, why, and how? But never being able to settle upon the biblical findings as the only adequate answers for truth! God: is indeed when, why, and for sure He is how it all came to be! Genesis 1:1; John 1:1; Hebrews 11: 6;

It is so unintelligent for us as created people to raise questions and to believe that we can set platforms disgracefully, for doubt to comfortably rest upon through science, while disdaining the scripture of the written bible.

Having been given the ability to physically examine the tangible things in and of the earth which leave no question that the things of our earthly existence could not have been in existence without the creative design of God; it is for sure that no man ever created them nor set them in the places where we found them!

It is God, who indeed, has given to us as mankind the ability to manipulate and to develop the skill to manage and to maintain dominance over all that has been created in the earth's realm.

To question, as to whether God should be excluded from the equations of reasoning to determine if it were ever a possible reality of God being the responsible creative designer, and the placement designator of all of things that He created, is forever unwarranted. Genesis 1:1; I Timothy 6:20;

The real questions ought to be why it is that human beings are the primary chosen created beings in the earth as it relates to having the power of control and manipulative skill! Specifically to do what other living created beings could never do. Genesis 1:26-28;

All uncertainty and inability lie within the makeup of man being the lesser created beings in the Cosmos, just a little lower than the angels. Although we are for sure the greatest of all created beings in the earth!

We are to manifest the glorified power and the spirit of God, which we carry about in our natural bodies. In the heart and super-conscience of the spirit-man on the inside of our own natural beings.

Most people of these latter generations are scientifically instructed and influenced to question everything, and to believe nothing; much rather not to accept anything as truth/true/proof, unless that it can't be scientifically disproved. True enough, you cannot get an answer if you never ask a question!

So, my question to you is; "why do you ask questions and continue compounding with more questions, even after you have been supplied and given the answers? Refusing to accept the source of the given answers seeking another source?"

Most people of the religious communities at large are consistently suggesting that there must be a God; somewhere? Only the bible tells us that He is the God whose throne is Heaven! Where He is; and presently He is right now in the earth, with us, but in us through salvation of Christ Jesus.

He can be found if you would just seek Him according to the written word of God. He won't be found according to selfish sinful and wicked agendas, or of any demoniacally influenced ideas, for the sake of human aggrandizement.

We are very quick to congratulate and to reward our humanness for the capture of our find and for the thrill of the hunt! Which led us to locate the objects that we had found.

We have been given the right; prerogative; thinking ability; and even intellectual yearnings to search for things and the very present cognition to recognize when we had indeed found what we were searching for. Having respect for our own intelligence; we diligently take the possession of the things that we have found as result of our own desperate search. Often as the invaluable prize of our possessions.

Daily, there is the struggle to reverence and to celebrate God for who He is, and for all that He has done for us in the earth. And for all that He has done for us as human beings. To many people living among us of these latter times, these days, celebrating God has become total foolishness!

We don't continue looking through the lenses of the binoculars or of the scope of the rifle in our hands, asking ourselves if we are sure it's exactly the right prey that we are supposed to be hunting, refusing to pull the trigger of the rifle. Rather we are assuredly determined not to allow the prey in our gun sights to escape being taken as the trophy of our hunting expedition.

It is not the common behavior that such an instance should occur, that we would have failed to accept the fact that taking the prize of the hunt is all in our hands. Disregarding the skills that we had acquired to be a hunter. Intelligence tells us that it is the prey that we desire and that we need to take the shot when we have spotted the prey that we are hunting.

We know that we are alive and living on the face of the planet and are totally aware of the fact that we did not get here on our own! The anatomy of the human body is so sophisticated, that no other human being could have ever been the one responsible for creating it!

Aside from the creative plan of God's designed process of procreation for mankind to continue replenishing the earth, only God could have ever been responsible. Knowing the physical traits which differ between the man and the woman; male and female. Even as every individual on the planet is different in one way or another, we are individually unique!

Although the birthing process is a miracle and an awesomely amazing creative method; no one from an outward position of control; not even a physician had been given the

authority to reach into the birth canal at each trimester of the pregnancy to construct the skeletal frame putting each bone in place. Neither were the parents given the powerful authority to construct the facial configuration of the babe in the womb.

Ain't nobody God; but God! He is the God of every blood kind; from the most extreme brute beast of the jungle and in the sea, to the very minuscule insects upon the earth that fly in the air, and crawl on top of, and underneath the ground.

We know this truth to be sound, yet we allow questions relative to our own humanness as to whether we were truly formed from the dust of the ground as the bible says that we were.

Most people prefer a life that doesn't answer to anyone ever! I have come to realize that it is not at all our own human existence that people are constantly in question of; they question the authority of the scripture.

Which tell us of the expected behavior to be carried out about in our human bodies. It is preferable that we make our own decisions, unaccounted for when we do things, and of how we go about getting those things done.

Those who are constantly in question here in the earth about everything; they are often found to be determined to turn the power of God; against Him; if it were possible to do so.

People are often found entertaining the subject of God, crossing over into the popular court of human opinion. Spending the bulk of their time questioning God, rather than obeying God, according to His Written word.

People are taught erroneously, to take their own given time of being here on the face of the earth for granted, though often unintentionally!

They say within themselves, what if I can do this and that without God's influence or without the help of the Lord?

Suppose I could live my life without caring or concern about what the bible has to say about the things that I choose to do with my life daily?

Well; what if I go about making the types of choices that are clearly against what the written word says that I ought to do and speak?

What would things be like if God could be eliminated?

You can always successfully erase the idea of thinking to acknowledge God; but you can never even approach the reality of God; desiring to erase God!

Have you not ever realized that as people die by the scores and leave the presence of this world, that God is still here! He is alive and doing as well as He always has? It's the subject of God; that appear at the demise of all human beings. God; has been there at all your funerals; have you ever been present at God's funeral?

These are just a few examples of the types of things that people are wondering about in their minds, on a consistent basis that have been suggested here.

These are the types of mental exercises that are most dangerous to the mentality of very curious people. Too busy selfishly determining to entertain such unhealthy thought patterns, they are responsible for the personal destruction of their own peace and tranquility.

No individual on the face of this planet should ever want to erase God from the reality of living. It is self-destructive to try and to disregard God. There is not anything on the face of the planet that God is not responsible for creating. There is absolutely nothing that we need to live each day that God has not provided!

Whenever we as faith-filled bible believing people, resist and aggressively refuse the influence of carnal thinking people, and the reasons that they choose to resist and to reject the written word of God; they are quick to remind us of their ed-

ucation! And how smart and efficient they are at researching biblical history, and the human characteristics of the people reported in scriptural accounts.

They want us to know and to believe that they have not arrived at the information that they have about the bible, just on a whim. They are indeed smart enough to have developed objectionable thinking of the scriptures, through the aid of their own educated intelligence and skill of research.

They will even go as far as to inform us, of the fee that they paid to develop the use their minds, to think in the manner of which they now have, to stand in opposition to the written word of God.

It is not as wise or even as intelligent as you might have been taught to believe that it is, to think contrary thoughts that encourage rebellion to the will of God. Even for your own life! Just because you can think a thing, it should never be viewed as a rite of passage for permissive collapses of judgment, in your mind to irrationally contemplate, with the intent to follow through on destructive choices.

Extreme support is given for those who have been fore fronted, to take charge of closing out the authority of the scriptures. So that mankind is allowed to live and to do and think as they are pleased to do so. That is dangerously outrageous among us!

Not that they have been able to disprove that God; is the ever; all Omnipotent; deity who rules the world; but rather that they have gone above and beyond to finally have the certified boldness to openly defy the truth about God!

Many have been financially funded to travel the globe to explore the earth digging and excavating historical ruins and celebrating their finds as discoveries? Only, they never have the wherewithal to also reveal the responsible culprit who planted the articles of their finds.

They just want all of us to know that they found them buried there beneath the earth! And the estimated time of just how long ago that it must have been, that the thing of their findings might have been buried there.

Discovered; or rather it has been uncovered and revealed. Someone dug it up; whatever has been found, has been exposed from its place of having been hidden away from man in the earth. The truth is that it got there somehow? Something or someone put it there? Not many are willing to admit and or even to conclude that hiding a thing always precedes the thing being found!

The psycho-analytical constitution of discovery has got many people inflated in their egos, to think and to almost believe that they can look and or dig anywhere they choose to do so. There are just too many places in the earth that are shut out from being able to dig into or to search on the bottom levels of their rest to get to the bottom to know what makes them exist and what gives the authority to flourish in the earth.

It has not been given to mankind to find that which had never been hidden or otherwise intentionally obscured from us? Finding and or a discovery is not even possible until we at least know or have an idea of what we are looking for.

With that being said, it is however, a discovery for those who unearthed those things that they never intended to look for! It was an accidental find. Life in and of itself is not built around stumbling upon things and accidentally seeing the reality of things we have landed upon that were once hidden from us.

Lots of curious people like to believe that life sort of rotates and circulates in the fashion of secret and unexpected finds, accidentally! While we're living by the divine intention of God's purpose for humanity in the earth.

Common sense should allow for us to think that since God created us and placed us above the ground, that everything that He intended for us to live successful on the earth, is also likewise above the ground with us! We dig beneath the earth and search for the things that are not exposed to us, all on the strength of desiring to have them above the ground with us!

Such thinking strongly suggests to us that life in and of itself was never supplied with any meaning of it's on to intentionally guide the direction that we should go about to reach our own given destinations. It most certainly suggest that we are to personally be responsible for giving any such purpose to the lives that we are living, through the written word of God.

That which had indeed been given to us was done so for us with intended designations and substantiated reasoning to be supported as personal gifts. God; never gives gifts for no reason at all; just because; or because He may want to show us how to avoid being idle in the earth?

No; we were given a purpose for the usage of the things, being gifted to extract the many usages and the benefits hidden on the inside of the things in the earth.

Of all of the uses of the citrus fruit that man has discovered along the way; somebody has got to stop and acknowledge that the multi-purposes of the fruit had already been created in the fruit. We never put the multi-dimensional aspects of the usage of the oils and the juices of the fruit, into the fruit.

However, when enough time was spent in research and exploration of the fruit it was soon discovered, that there was indeed so much more that could be done with the fruit of the trees other than just to eat them.

All of the things that we have discovered in the usage of the fruit have been greatly beneficial for the aid of all mankind. Corporations, and farmers might have taken it upon themselves to lay the claim to the discovery in the usage of the fruit; but it was God who made the fruit what it is from the beginning.

Even though it had been also intended for mankind, by

God; that we look deeply enough into the fruit, to discover all that there is to be found. Acknowledgment is necessary to be given to those who did apply the necessary research to discover the awesomeness of the fruit.

Millions of others have also had their hands on the fruit for multiples of reasons that never had the wherewithal to even begin to think that there just might be more to be realized than what meets the eyes. However too many finders have stood in their own way likewise becoming losers amid their own successful finds.

The given acknowledgment for having found the thing is one reality; however, taking the credit for the actual thing that was found is another reality all together. So, the questions become; "did you hide the thing there, or did you find the thing hidden there?"

Finding the thing should be enough for those who have indeed found the hidden thing in its hiding place. Only too many people would much rather be recognized as the more significant one, who may have been responsible for the thing being in that place from the beginning.

Many of the manufactures are extremely cocky, in that they have the nerve to suggest that they are responsible for certain fruit that are in the produce sections of the stores now. They hired scientist to genetically split seeds, cross germinating them on the strength of their own curiosity, to recreate a product that never previously existed. The results have not all been suitable for human consumption!

Their farmers who grow the produce are experimenting with many different types of pesticides and chemicals for the mass producing their product, at much faster growth rates, that also produce more product than normal. As a result, we are experiencing more product recall because of illness and of death even because of the genetic interference and experimental growth rate.

All of the major networks are consistently reporting of another recall and the damage that the product has been reported to have done to the consumers across the country. And of certain farming regions where the products had been mass produced.

Laboratory scientists, who suggest that the animal consumption of foods should be the exact same quality to that of human consumption, have experimented for years on rats and apes, and many other types of animals; testing the chemicals in the new products?

"But Daily People Fight for the Right to Choose?"

It's an ongoing saga daily, whereas people are standing against any form of prohibitionist who maintains the right as well as the heart to regulate how the populist, who make up the churches, ought to allow for their minds to think.

Stand-up comics and political activist are now involved in the aggravated dialogue of taking away the control of the influence of the churches to allow for people to think and to live exactly as they choose to do so.

So many people are no longer ashamed to allow for their minds to wonder and to float through empty space, though destination-less, having no intended purpose for the expedition of their mental travel.

They allow anyone who has a contrary idea or condescending theory of who they have been taught or have decided within their own minds of the reality of God; to speak into their ability to reason. Our people of the earth no longer have the fear of God in their hearts and their minds.

Most people nowadays are choosing excitement over and above truth and reality. To them it really doesn't matter that "God"; is God of the entire Universe. If they can influence the idea of thought about God being something or someone other than what has been written in the Holy Bible; that is what they are going with as an element of truth in their own minds.

Many people really do still believe that God is God; they are just not afraid to sin against God anymore. People are not afraid to disappoint God; or to break the heart of God because of their foul behavior. Hebrews 6:4-6

If you could change the color of your own skin and lose consciousness over their determination to redefine God; it will never influence their hearts or cause them to change their ways of thinking about the Lord. I think that they are rather overwhelmed with the idea of being let out to the pasture to roam free of their own thinking. To decide for themselves who God just ought to be? It needs to be established that people need to get over themselves, before they eventually blow their own minds!

While it is understood that people are their own bosses; or rather they are personally responsible for the manner of which they reason with their own minds and of the conclusions in which they mentally arrive to establish their own foundations for living; the design from the beginning of time has been that men would have someone to guide them in regulating their choices of thought matter.

My friend it is necessary that those people who have been awarded the benefit of thought before you and I ever came along to this earth to live, that they instruct us in the matters of understanding our "Father; and our Lord, Jesus Christ;" of which we would soon come into contact with.

I am not at all suggesting that we be slave-like little drones and clones of everyone else's opinions of thinking, whereas we have absolutely no grasp on our own abilities to think for ourselves. But, I am concerned that we ought to be more receptive to the teaching and to the instructions of those who have already experienced the benefits and the enhancements of living, as result of the knowledge received through the written word of God.

As I, myself, have been informed; the written word of God is to be experienced much more so, than just to be lectured and listened to in a classroom setting. No one will even know the truth of the actuality of God's word through listening and hearing only.

The instruction of the word must be received in the heart and then applied to our actions. And to our daily regimen of going about doing things which define for others, of just who we really are. The book of James; instruct us that we ought to be doers of the word of God, and not just hearers only. [James 1:22]

I am convinced that the world would be a much better place to live, if the people of every society were allowed to see the word of God lived through the people of the churches. Rather than just heard as a sermonic delivery over the pulpit in the churches. Far too many of the preachers themselves are inquisitively curious, which causes a hindrance to the delivery of the messages that they bring to the churches.

It is obvious to the people in attendance, when the messenger is doubtful and in question of the message that they are attempting to deliver to the people. Nowadays, most of the people in the pews are educated and intellectual; they are often already informed and convinced in their own minds.

Having a determination to never be influenced to think differently, otherwise. Between Sunday services, they are venturing out into all sorts of discoveries of information and ideas of the existence of our world of living; and of how it all came to be.

There is now the outrageous development of such biblical disregard and denigrating devalue of the word of God and the people of the clergy. As a result of some people; overlooking the fact that not everyone has been found to be guilty of fraudulent behavior in the churches.

So many people never had a desire to be governed by the word of God and the teachings of the churches. The exposure of some of the most disobedient and ungodly people in the churches has almost caused the spiritual demise for many among the religious communities of the churches.

Many have taken occasion to throw up both their hands to resolve that it is not worth it to try to live for God since His people appear to be no better-behaved than the rest of the sinful people in the world, who never have attended a church or had never confessed Christ as their Lord and Savior.

It is a much more common occurrence to watch the people of the churches, rather than to look through the written word of God seeking to find God; there! So many people of the churches that should be the living examples of Christ; have themselves become the dividing petitions to blind the potential seekers of God; obscuring their ability to know the love of God.

In all truth and fairness, the people of the secular society are not given the real chance to have their ideas about God closely evaluated, simply because the people who attend the churches are not really the living witnesses that the bible calls for. While the people don't mind being scientific, in that they have learned to question; and to doubt everything, they have simultaneously developed the refusal to be spiritual and holy in their manner of expression of living.

Amazingly, as people are discouraged to allow for the churches to influence their process of thinking, to maintain erect posture, as it relates to righteous behavior, clean hands; and purified thinking; Holy living according to the word of God; the unrighteous and the ungodly people are warring to influence the people to be the total opposite of what is required of the people who are planning and expecting to go to Heaven to live with the Father; forever!

We are made to feel as if we have arrived at a certain level

of maturity whenever we reveal that we are capable of thinking for ourselves, in respect of making our own decisions. "Thinking for yourselves" is often the message that is sent in opposition, against the teachings of the churches. To those who think favorably and faithfully on the Lord; our God; they are said to have been brainwashed and deceived for having accepted the truth of the written word of God.

I am saying daily; Lord Jesus; wash my mind with the truth of your word, and you ought to also ask for the Lord to wash your mind! If this is your reference to being brainwashed, my friends I am guilty indeed!

It has been suggested that the participation of Yoga – Blanketing the Mind; sitting in total silence, while thinking on nothing and no one; that it has far more reaching benefits than fasting and prayer?

Yet no one have been proven to have been healed through the practice of Yoga; many others have the testimony of being healed and totally set free from sickness and diseases, through praying and fasting. They are healed to this very day and have never been sick ever again.

I do know that I felt accepted as an adult whenever the older more mature people of mine own surroundings experienced my ability to think and to make what I thought at the time were sound decisions. Although many of the decisions that I made were later determined not to have been sound decisions after all; they were the decisions that I wanted to make on my own!

As we reach the age of accountability, we have no problem of letting other grown individuals know that we are also grown now! It is more-so the desire of the average individual to think on their own and much less desirable to be told what and how to think.

Even as the young adults that we were; when being criticized for having made the wrong decisions and having done the wrong things; we were quick with the vengeance to say to others that they ought to let us make the mistakes that come with maturing and becoming an adult; after all everyone makes mistakes?

Many people of today, would much rather be wrong by their own will and volition than to have someone else lead them and guide them into being right, and living by the righteous design of the teachings of the bible. However; making mistakes and some bad decisions is not at all the focus of this particular topic of discussion!

"They'd Rather Be Lost and Unfounded?"

Used to be the time when the people of the churches wanted the leadership of the churches to tell them what to do; they wanted to be taught how to regulate their own thinking process; they wanted to be led in decision making skills?

It's just that the secular influences of the society ran into to brick wall like resistance when launching attempts at speaking to the minds and to the intellects of the people of the churches who were more-so donned the people of faith in God.

As a result of not being at all very appreciative of the fact that the people of the churches were not at all influenced to doubt the truth of the bible and of the truth and the reality of God; the average people of the churches were labeled as being closed minded.

During the days and the times of the closed mindedness of the people of the churches; there was much less of the reported accounts of crimes and of abusive behavior among the people in the churches and of the societies.

Family living was much more respected, desired, and even stronger, having values that made for better communities and schools, much better working environments, and cleaner television and entertainment. You could walk into a church service and know the presence of God among the people who were there.

Many of the things that we are seeing on today's platforms of living and the behavioral aspects of many people; like mindedness of back in the days of stricter living and godly thinking and influence are strongly debated and heavily resisted by the people of the leadership aspect in the secular society and in many of the local churches.

People just did not do and say any and everything that they thought that they wanted to, simply because there were limits and established boundaries in their minds and in the meditation of their thinking processes.

Now I know there is a vast percentage of the population today that will come forth to debate the fact that people had better thinking processes back in the earlier times of living. Someone suggested to them that they had the right to think whatever they wanted to think and to explore other possibilities of behaving and of living as an individual. Someone came forth to let the people off the hook; so to speak!

The strategic motivations and the wisdom of the people from the past generations was to get us in check early on, and to prevent the monster of our thinking to take hold on the inside of us and to be allowed to grow up with us to become just as grown as we would also become with age. Almost everything from the past generation's methodology of teaching and training; raising our families and child discipline has been targeted and challenged as offensive and abusive?

Three

"Anxious; Looking Too Hard To See!"

And when the messengers of John were departed, he began to speak unto the people concerning John, What went ye out into the wilderness for to see? A reed shaken with the wind? But what went ye out for to see? A man clothed in soft raiment? Behold, they which are gorgeously appareled, and live delicately, are in kings' courts. But what went ye out for to see? A prophet? Yea I say unto you, and much more than a prophet. [St John 7:24-26]
Be careful for nothing; but in everything by prayer and supplication with thanksgiving let your request be made known to God. [Philippians 4:6]

Anxiously Driven to Look but, Always Failing to See!

Anxiety ~ Feeling of worry -nervousness or agitation, often about something that is going to happen; something that worries somebody-a subject or concern that causes worry; a strong wish to do something-especially if the wish is unnecessarily or unhealthily strong; extreme apprehension.

Psychiatry ~ a medical condition marked by intense apprehension or fear of real or imagined danger... {Encarta Dictionary; English North America}

I can tell you that more often than realized, curiosity is the breeding grounds for anxiety. It's what drives us so desperately to look more deeply beyond what we might have already visualized.

Even though there may be no real vested interest in what it is that we desire to see. Many are determined to just keep looking even though they have come to the end of the road, where at that very moment there is nothing left for them to see.

Curiosity is that "just because I want to" type of an element that fuels the spirit of anxiety, which tells them they shouldn't be denied the opportunity to see, just as everyone else sees. So many people seek to tie a knot in the need to know and "I just want to know" binding them together. Into the same necessarily important ability to acquire knowing things that are both available to be shared and the things that are indeed to be kept private!

A moment is all it takes to both cause and allow an accident that could also be life threatening. Just on the outside of the moving vehicle that we are riding and moving forward in, there is always something happening that could take away our necessity to be focused when we allow it. As a driver, the one thing that I have always seemed to pay attention to, was that after many car wrecks had happened the drivers reported that they looked away for only a moment?

At the scene of a crime or an accident, the officials that arrive to handle the incident are often heard telling the people in the crowd that came around to see what happened to "get back!" The spectators in the crowd are often very agitated and emotionally stirred to the point that they may even create another sense of danger unrelated to the situation that had already taken place. The curiosity of the people in the crowd is so heightened that it appears that the people are deaf and cannot hear instructions?

Sometimes the people are so driven to see what happened, that the law officers may be forced to draw their service weapons to encourage compliance among the crowd. The people are convinced that they need to see for themselves what has taken place at the scene of this particular incident. They are not going to accept the idea that they don't need to see the very devastating sight of the situation.

Coming up in the church, they used to say to us; "if you catch on fire the world will come and watch you burn!" They thought that they were telling us very spiritual information until years later we are noticing that the same people that were purportedly watching us as we burned with the Holy Ghost, that they are still on the sidelines looking too hard to actually see! They never saw the need to likewise catch on fire and burn themselves' with the Holy Ghost; they're still looking.

The misnomer was that we were to get other people to see what we are doing? We need most definitely to get other people to do what we are doing and to become who we are in the Kingdom of the Lord!

As a blood washed believer, in the Lord; seeing me do what the word of the Lord commands for us to do, won't help the next individual, except that they are watching to see me as an example. So the question swiftly becomes, What are they looking for initially? We all must be obedient doers of the word of God for ourselves, in order to reap the benefit of God's blessings and eternal reward!

Just think with me, there are more people who watch the games as they are played, than there is of those who actually play the game. In a sense, we are too often attempting to entice people of the churches, to be game watchers, when they ought to be engaged on the field of play. (Figuratively speaking)

In essence, we are being taught to be church house actors and pretenders. We should be strongly encouraged to be the people who are real true living epistles of Christ's examples, for them to see. There is a very strong difference between being a true witness and an actor that know what people want to see; big difference!

The real dilemma that has hit the churches, is that everybody wants to get a good seat in the sanctuary, so that they can see what's taking place. People come to the church looking for lots of things to happen, but hardly a few of the people actually come watching for the move of God!

People who go to the church, even on a regular basis, are not necessarily people who study the bible and pray to enter into a relationship with the Father in Heaven. They are underestimated as being the same people that are able to show forth the powerful presence and the love of God.

Being unprayerful and unfaithful to God, people have the tendency to bring the possibilities of ungodly situations with them into the sanctuary. All kinds of things are subject to happen under these circumstances. I have seen some of the craziest things happen in the sanctuary of the churches. Right in the midst, when the people are supposed to worshiping, people break out with all sorts of things that have nothing at all to do with worshiping God.

We can't stop things from happening! As it is life that is happening on cue, just as it's supposed to happen. It's left up to us to avoid allowing curiosity on the inside of us, to drive us to have to see what is happening, just because we are curious to know.

It can be the difference between what will always be regarded as a wise decision and a foolish gesture. We are aware of the many people who are already in the grave? As result of the fact that they wanted to see what was happening!

I don't know that it is that thing happening that was so unforgivable to cause the curious individual to suffer the tragedy, or if it was indeed the curiosity; or both in simultaneity?

Many might try and justify, by saying that if there was nothing happening, there would be no reason to be curious? Now I know that most of you were taught, just as I was also taught, to simply mind your own business!

Some would think that to simply keep it moving is in many instances to be uncaring of others. However, my friend to be caring and to be curious, are two totally different things also.

In school I was in the Concert Band and the Chorus; both of these musical choices required us to read music charts. The one thing that I discovered very quickly was that when you failed to keep your eyes on the music chart, almost immediately you would lose your place on the chart. Keeping up with the music chart and following along as we played the music are not to be thought of as looking, but while thinking and focusing in another place all together.

My instrument could become the one instrument to foul up the whole musical selection. There was no way for me to do my part in the band, wondering off mentally. A metronome could be used to keep time, but to look away allowing for something else to take away our attention, caused us to lose the timing of the music.

As things are always moving at a rate that suggest that we

see it right now, by the time that we looked in the direction of the things happening many times we had already missed it.

At times we may be so obviously observant that we can feel that we are about to see something take place? We may feel that we are looking ahead to actually see what is about to take place. Under these circumstances it is to be assumed that most people are always looking for the wrong things to take place.

Curiosity seeks for the excitement and the interesting things. Curious people are often bored with the necessary things of life that they are required to set their sights upon. I am of the opinion that you can be too curious to realize you're anxious, or for sure you can be thoroughly hindered from knowing of the cause of your anxiety.

Many people of the churches who are indeed anxious to move forward, they are not always equipped to focus on the faith and the word of God that is required to complete the assignment that they are driven to undertake. Many people who do indeed mean well, don't always do well, looking to a goal that they will never faithfully see.

Curiosity will cause you to think of yourself as being capable to do certain things that you have never been trained or developed to do. Curiosity will often expose the immaturity and the insecurity about you that you were not even aware of.

Being curious you may often find yourself jumping out ahead of the right timing of the move of God. You're looking to see things move! You're looking for things to explode into manifested realities! Only to be confounded and what I will refer to as being stupefied, as a result.

The real truth is that many people that appear to be rather settled and calm, they are driven on the inside of themselves and in total unrest. To be motivated to do certain things in this life may often be a very good thing. To become your motor mechanism that internally motivates you to go forward is not always a good thing.

Sometimes, the signification to you is that you need to stand motionless to the situation at hand. There are times when the best thing to do will be to do nothing at all!

Growing up back in the 60's and 70's, the circus was really a big thing then. The State Fair was equally a major attraction to the inquisitive minds of the people. Curiosity will cause everything that you get involved with to become a circus and a freak show.

Being so driven to see things that you are determined to show others that you saw, is when you may become a side show to the people that know you? They just may not be as interested in what you are seeing or of what it is that you can report that you saw.

Never forget the fact that other people can and will see for themselves when interested. It is a serious error to want to be the eyes for everyone else! God never called for you to be security system for the people of the Kingdom of God.

Even when you have been the witness to what may indeed be detrimental to the people of God; many of the people may turn a deaf ear and blind eye to your admonition or warning.

Some people just simply don't care about hearing the report of what you have seen, where you saw it, or who it was that was doing whatever it was that you saw; they don't care!

Then there are those people who make a living so to speak; of the thing that you purport to see. They may prefer to you as a buffoon or a clown, as you go out of your way to convince other people that you were the one who saw whatever you might have seen.

Those who pretend to be so excited or carried away with your report could even be setting you up in some way for the greatest fall of your life. You might need to consider the fact that everything that you report to have seen is not necessarily what you saw!

People would come from all over the state and even beyond to see the attractions of the State Fair, that would prove to be only attractive ideas of the things advertised to be seen. I can remember being very disappointed at the actual image of the thing that we were supposed to see. Because it wasn't exactly what we were told that it would be.

Some things were only fake mannequins, replicas of the things we expected to see. Others were only stilled photographs of the things that we had expected to see. They didn't always have the actual images of the objects which made up the headlines of the attractions.

Most of the things were determined to have never been real. They bated us all in to get our money on the basis of our own driving curiosity, to go and see for ourselves. Of course they knew that only those who were indeed curious would come out and see the purported attraction!

"Fascinated With What You Saw?"

Some people are really fascinated whenever they see people go beyond the boundaries, just across the barriers into the forbidden. Simple people are blown away at the nerves and the gall of certain people who have no respect for rules or guidelines.

Just to see them go all of the way out to break the laws and to show no concern for their own behavior, is rather exciting to some people. You need to understand that if indeed you are willing to supply a show of yourselves, there are many people that are also willing to watch the show, all of the way to the destructive end of your fiasco!

Curiosity encourages one to jump over the fence seeking an entrance at the rear, rather than to ring the doorbell and enter at the front door. It is that kind of mentality which seeks to search out the deep dark dirty mysterious underground details.

People want to know about the filth and stench of sin and of Satan. They want to seriously know what makes dirt dirty; what makes filth so filthy? They want to know why it is that the most beautiful things are not quite as appreciated in the dark?

The things that most people simply accept as the truth, other more curious people refuse to accept the quickest answers as just because it is so. But you must know that those who are most curious are not always the quickest to jump into things.

They sort of want to know from a distance; or better yet they might prefer to know because you tried it first. The powerful strength of success has always been constructed on the truthful relevance of the curiosity in the minds of people.

Entertainment is very powerful; even as it has swept its way into the churches, because people are interested in being able to say that they saw something! Most people in the churches are not at all seeking the Lord to be powerfully filled and empowered with the Holy Ghost!

But, they do want to see other powerful people at the church. Even in the secular world, they may not desire to be the entertainers, but they are consistently working to afford the ticket price tag, for being entertained.

The movie making and film industry, have developed films so much so now, that it seems as if you can walk right up to the screen and shake hands with the characters in the movie. Animated films are amazing, cartoon characters do things that we never imagined that would ever be able to do. Television and film technology is so advanced now all because of the fact that people are now more curious than ever before.

Movie Theaters, are advanced to another level to parallel certain restaurants where you can dine while watching your favorite movie. They know that since people want to see, not only will we give them something to see, we will also supply a taste for their taste buds, while watching the film.

Entertainment is now in full bloom; they have reclining beds and comfortable couches to rest on while the movie is playing. Seeing a movie has become a complete experience; you will walk away from there excited about what you have seen for sure!

Gas service stations are now equipped with television monitors, whereas you can actually view a few moments of the news on CNN & FOX news networks while you pump your gas.

Talk about the fascination of seeing; Lowe's is now selling a refrigerator that has a full video screen on the front door. The video is equipped to show you all sorts of things depending on the package that you purchase.

The one thing that the world is sure of these days is that people are driven to see all kinds of things. Some funeral homes in certain cities have now what they are referring to as "Drive By; funerals" of which is a bit much for me.

Television cameras are in the operating rooms; Court rooms; Class Rooms; all other sorts of venues that never used to have such activities. And of course the television cameras are almost dominating the sanctuaries of the churches.

Many people have decided against going out to the services at the local church, they are satisfied to watch church service on the television and or on the computer screen. They are determined to believe that just as long as they are able to see what's going on at the church they are complete in the service that they have decided to give to the Lord; or not?

The leadership of the churches is guilty of causing the idea of the church to be shifted from doing the work of the Lord to just seeing it as the experience! You never really know just how beautiful being in the church services used to be, until things all changed whereas the people are no longer there.

Scandal after scandal, have ripped through the church communities across the board. Detrimentally, people have always been curious as to whether or not the confessing people in the churches were as real as they confess to be in the Lord. As I mentioned earlier in this chapter, people who came to watch and to see, had been captured and trapped in the midst, and are still only watchers and lookers!

The fact that most people are looking for whose to blame for not being successful at being able to reach beyond the driven curiosity of the people. This has given added reasoning to strengthen those who have not decided to make being saved and serving the Lord with their lives, the ultimate choice.

When only looking, one has not the power to see beyond the show! Neither is there compassion to recognize the needed help of the Lord to change individuals behavior and choices for lifestyles. As result, they see the open errors in the people at the local churches. They see living activity among people which does not at all reflect the mandate of the scripture.

You might want to consider the fact that blind wolves neither can see the sheep. Even though they hear the bleating of the sheep in the congregations. They know that they are there, but because they have even gone nose blind also, they cannot detect the true scent of the sheep. There is too many wolves in the midst of the sheep.

Even when the wolves among the churches uprise, causing all sorts of dramatic outbreaks in the midst of what ought to be the peaceful fellowship of the sheep, lookers and watchers who have never been converted, born again, blood washed by Christ Jesus, they have no discernment! They are convinced that the people of the churches normally act this way.

They are also looking on as the leadership in many of the churches drop the ball in renegade support on known wolves who are seated in the pews, haven thrown their punches, but are now hiding their hands, sitting on them. They had been looking at the leadership witnessing those wolves destroy the sheep, all while they preferred not to protect nor to retaliate!

They are looking at leaders that they can't see nor discern that they are not even surrendered to the leading of the Lord themselves. Yes, they're looking, steadfastly affixed on what other people are doing! But are missing the fact that they are becoming, or that they have already become what they are looking at, in who they are looking at.

You must be able to see your own heart and the spirit of which you are operating in, as you are looking at other people! The question is, who are you? Through your observation, you have an idea of who other people just might be, but you do know for sure who you are! You may not even like who and what you see whenever you look into the mirror, but you know that you're looking at your reflection!

You need to come to grips with why you are so curious with other people. You need to know why it is that you just need to know their personal business. I'd like to say it like so, "Reel Your Own Nose Into Your Own Business!" Stop fishing for everyone else's information. Better chances are that your life in definitely more interesting than their's!

Monster Among Us; Curiosity........

Four

Curiosity of Fossils; [Who]~? Put It There

Fossils; in the spirit of my own revelatory comprehensive mind; are the unearthed deceptive geological finds as result of the ageless old disfigured and even Mal-figured created dinosaur images of satanic thoughts and ideas. A~P.~W.T.J. 2023

Greater Answers Than We Have Ever Been Given

After having been formed, from the imaginative ideas of their own Satanic illustrator; their gigantic enormous life forms failed to live and to successfully roam the earth. They were indeed domineering and destructive in the earth, though it was indeed short lived. They were hungry and angry destroyers killing and devouring one another. Much sooner than science would like to imagine, there would be only one species left upon the face of the earth. The story of dinosaurs reveal no since of devotion or comradery to suggest that preservation of life would ever be realized among them.

The actuality of the finding of fossils can not be declared as a lie, simply because a lie will never produce any manifested evidence. However, the idea of fossils having literally been found in the earth, can be understood and better realized to be one of the greatest deception ever manifested in all the realm of the earth and humanity!

God had already purposed the gift of life, and the rightful authority and ability of walking upright on two legs and the geographical knowledge of roaming the earth to mankind. The intellectual compass on the inside of man, would not let them roam in one direction, only never to find their way back to where they began their journey.

As the earth was the given domain for God's creations, God erased dinosaurs from the face of the earth! Satan has been trying to erase mankind from the face of the earth also, but he has failed and will continue to fail.

Fossils are the clearer indication of Satan's failure when putting his own devilish attempt at creation. I am sure that many might be thinking, if he did it back then, why isn't he still doing it now? I'm a witness of Satan doing things and fleeing the scene. Upon his return, his plans are to do something other than what had already been done before.

Even when he does return with the very same packages, he is seeking new prey to levy his attack upon them. The greater probability is that he never intended to perpetuate his idea, as much as that he was more interested in proving that it could be done by him.

Have you ever read anywhere in the scriptures about Satan's ability to remember what he had done to you? He may indeed recognize his own evil works upon seeing for the second time, but he is a stubborn, hard headed, determinant thief and destroyer who could care-less to remember.

Remembering what has been done often brings remorse and the need for repentance, to which Satan is eternally incapable of doing. So whatever he has done lacks the fixation of permanence and perpetual continuance.

Satan is not and has never been a creator! He's a duplicator and imitator! Only God has the blueprint for life forms that are living on the earth.

God intended for man to rule in the earth not untamable beast! Devouring creatures, with teeth as large as to that of bricks, and over sized disk or cylinders. It has never been the intention of God for mankind to be eaten up and devoured in the earth! As it would definitely signify that man no longer ruled in the earth, but had now been conquered themselves!

It would be horrible for all of mankind if the tables were to be turned whereas the animals would have the dominion and the power over all of the earth. I am of the opinion that this is the reason that God allowed for dinosaurs to become extinct; wiped out from the face of the earth.

While science sort of celebrates that dinosaurs were the most devastating beast that ever walked the planet; it was God's plan for man to dominate and to rule over all that would dwell on the face of the planet.

Dinosaurs; or better referred to as the "Terrible Lizards of the earth" would have been here devouring God's greatest creation of the earth had they been allowed to roam the planet.

There is no way that man and dinosaur could have ever been allowed to co-exist in the earth. God makes no mistakes, even as He allowed for the dinosaurs to be gone from the earth and from this historical era in time.

Whenever a fossil has been unearthed, through discovery and digging, we know that it has been in the earth for decades, and even for centuries. Nothing new about the fossils that are discovered. They are age old deteriorating remains from an error so far away from any era that is accurately known to man. No flesh or blood discovered, just dried out bones.

Satan; however, is older than the ages of both time and man, being that he was created to be an eternal spirit being. While time rolls on forwards and ticks away minute by the minute, eternity exists without the necessary measurement of or the movement of time. No weeks, no months, no years, no decades, no centuries, and no millenniums!

Therefore as Satan was already here to see God place the measurement of time into the reality of the earth's creation, it is no struggle for me to see how that he was there during the dinosaur period and era of existence on the earth. God and all of Heaven's creations are before the earth's existence.

Satan who became a mischievous misfit in the Kingdom of Heaven, was cast down to the earth's atmosphere, away from the immediate presence of God. He was never left alone to do whatever he wanted to do in the earth. However, he is the prince of the air and of darkness.

In Heaven he had an assignment around the throne of God. He had things literally to do among the host of Heaven. He was cast down from Heaven yet with all of the tools and the princely authority that he had in Heaven, though he no longer had anything to do with it.

He was sent away with nothing left to do. Remember in his heart he wanted to be what he could not be and would never ever be, which was God; or greater than God! He is the unemployed enemy of all creation! His determination has always been to have things his way, if at all possible!

It is fair to say that he put his hands to an idea to create and to form a species of his own in the earth. As like unto God's master creation and earthly formation of mankind in the earth. But it is also most necessary to acknowledge the fact the he failed at his own work and prototype!

Seeing that Satan's ideas failed to produce a lasting suitable life-form in the earth, his greatest failure was to show that he was just as creative as the most high God? He was already a failure in that he was not able to have already been in existence. God created Lucifer and designed his spirit being for the host of Heaven.

As his desire has been to be like the most high God, to exalt his throne as high as the throne of God, he is still trying to wreak havoc on God's creation. Oh but he has failed, gravely! Seeing and knowing that man is buried in the ground after death, Satan chose to hide his failure in the ground; as result of their death!

Don't be fooled, Satan knows that he cannot hide anything from God! And neither can he successfully hide anything from the people of God, in the earth! But he can deceive those who choose to disregard God as the creator, and to trick them into believing that the story of creation is false and biblically bolstered.

God had already designed a spiritual life and a natural body form for man in the earth. Satan had been a citizen of heaven at one time; {Ezekiel 28:}. He had knowledge of God's plan for such a created being in the earth. He being somewhat like the Apostle Paul with the exception to having a natural body of flesh and bones; he had been there before in the presence of God.

Paul, said in the

> FOR WE KNOW THAT THE LAW IS SPIRITUAL: BUT I AM CARNAL SOLD UNDER SIN.   ROMANS 7:14:

Satan knew that God's initial plan for mankind was done in the spirit before it ever became a natural thing. God went to the drawing board within Himself; and drew up the blueprint for forming man in the natural.

So in his futile recognition of the alarming fact that he was never going to be like God in heaven or in the earth, he begins to acknowledge the fact that he is damned under sin forever! Preventing him from successfully creating anything in the earth. Knowing that the earth and all that is on the face of the earth, belongs to God.

> THE EARTH IS THE LORD'S AND THE FULLNESS THEREOF, THE WORLD, AND THEY THAT DWELL THEREIN. PSALMS 24:1

> FOR TO WILL IS PRESENT WITH ME; BUT HOW TO PERFORM THAT WHICH IS GOOD I FIND NOT. ROMANS 7:18B

Satan knew that the making of mankind was a good thing as well as it was definitely a God thing! So there was never any attempt to make another man; but there was an attempt to make a creature that would precede the making of man! Bigger, more devastating to the given greater power and authority than to that of man in the earth.

> NOW IF I DO THAT I WOULD NOT, IT IS NO MORE I THAT DO IT, BUT SIN THAT DWELLETH IN ME. ROMANS 7:20

Satan, looks at what is coming out as a result of his work with disgust. But, also realizing that it is sin on the inside of him that produces such ugliness of imagination! Even he didn't want to be the one given the recognition for having been the creator such hideous fearful beast.

Thus we find the one who buried the hidden finds of the earth. For which we as mankind have not been successful assigning God "THE CREATOR;" as being the one who created such hideous evil beast upon the earth.

> I FIND THEN A LAW, THAT WHEN I WOULD DO GOOD, EVIL IS PRESENT WITH ME. ROMANS 7:21

Satan knows that everything that comes from God is definitely good! He's aware of the fact that mankind all over the face of the earth from the beginning up unto this present time, that they are going to marvel and give praise and thanksgiving for the things that God has done. He knows that mankind is going to worship the awesome splendor that belong to the work of God's own hands.

I hear Satan confessing here; in reference to the fact that everything that he tries to do that might be by a fraction of any percentage of what could ever be called good; that it turns out evil, outright ugly and wrong!

All of his good intentions turned out bad and hell bound! Just a gigantic enormous mess, that perhaps he thought that it might show himself to be like God also; as is mankind.

However, the all-knowing God; who is infinite in all of His wisdom; already knows the nature of Satan and his original cause to the descent of his own fallen hell bound status. Destined doubtless, for the eternal lake of burning fire and brimstone. His irreversible status and eternal sentencing doom have been eternally set, and cannot be reversed!

Of which is the cause of everything that is touched by Satan to fail, rot, and to eventually fossilize! Signifying the fact that it is permanently dead, and could have never had the chance of living. Having been an eternal failure from the instance of its own imaginative thought.

Satan being rejected of God; forever; can never produce anything that could ever be pleasing to God in any manner. The idea of fossilizing his imaginative mess, through hiding it in the ground, hoping for non-discovery, is exactly where men get the idea of trying to hide that mess of their lives as well!

Sinful man never equate the fact that their sneaky deceptive ideas for covering up their mess, as being originated by the initiator of sin. Sin and iniquity are the only thing that Satan successfully levied upon creation that is still alive and running rampant in the earth! Satan could be talking here:

FOR I WAS ALIVE WITHOUT THE LAW ONCE; BUT WHEN

THE COMMANDMENT CAME, SIN REVIVED, AND I DIED

ROMANS 7: 9

The Apostle Paul is writing to us explaining the plight of his own sinful experience and escapades in the flesh. Whereas sometimes it might have seemed impossible to overcome the will to sin outright in the flesh. But as for Paul, being a created man of God; by God; and for the glory of God; a remedy was and is still prepared for all mankind.

Remember now that the infamous Satan; use to be called Lucifer (son of the morning) who use to be in heaven with God. Living and enjoying the benefits of eternity in the presence of God. But his once blessing of eternity, is now an eternal curse!

He was truly alive in the realm of the spirit, wherein he did those things which pleased the Father! Until Lucifer's heart changed because of pride. The Father spoke against the pride in Lucifer's heart, thus creating the law against pride. For which sin would forever be alive in the eternal heart of Satan.

He has forever been declared the enemy of God! The evil deceiver and father of every lie, and a murderer from the beginning. Murderers always try and hide their kill to prevent being discovered; {dis-cover-ed}. Their determination is to prevent the lid from coming off of the evil done against another person.

Jesus; teaches the Jews,

YE ARE OF YOUR FATHER THE DEVIL, AND THE LUST OF THE FLESH YE WILL DO. HE WAS A MURDERER FROM THE BEGINNING, AND ABODE NOT IN THE TRUTH, BECAUSE THERE IS NO TRUTH IN HIM. WHEN HE SPEAKETH A LIE HE SPEAKETH OF HIS OWN: FOR HE IS A LIAR, AND THE FATHER OF IT.   ST. JOHN 8:44

Remember that a temporary plan of sin will cause a permanent sentence to hell! This is the reason that Satan has so overwhelmed mankind and caused them to think that perhaps God had hidden something from man in the earth.

Most people who want to know the truth about historical finds, have searched the scripture and have sort of held God suspect to the non-mention of the fossils discovered.

Why doesn't the bible mention dinosaurs? Many theologians and preachers have been delivering the message of the preeminent world, suggesting that perhaps dinosaurs ruled the earth until a cataclysmic collision of some sort of a meteor from out of space, crashed into the earth killing the then existing lifeforms of dinosaurs.

It is the divine plane of God for mankind to find the hidden works of Satan in the earth. But it was never the intention of God, for man to celebrate to the point that they have now ruled out the fact that God; is the God of all creation, and of all created beings!

THE EARTH IS THE LORD'S AND THE FULLNESS THEREOF; THE WORLD AND THEY THAT DWELL THEREIN.   PSALMS 24:1

The found fossilized skeletal remains of those creatures are so far away in style of any of the created beings in the earth since the time of creation. As we know of it from the standpoint and documentation of the biblical accounts of creation. (Genesis)

Most things that are common to the natural figuration of animalistic creations in the earth, are similarly recognized in many of the fossilized creatures that have been found. But, the exceptions of the dinosaurs configuration is the extreme measures of disproportionate sizes and measurement stature.

Satan, lacks the super intelligence of God! As the creator of all heaven and earth and all that dwell in the earth and in heaven. Therefore, he doesn't have the creative skill to build it for the inhabitance of the earth to share the dwelling of the earth as our earthly place of living.

In the discovery of fossils; it is paramount that we recognize Satan's determination to build it bigger and even more powerful than God! Isn't it amazing that the blood DNA of the dinosaurs has not at all been discovered as well? Of course deceived mankind; [scientist] would certainly make a scientific effort to bring to life once again, this once historical animalistic dominator!

It has not been until now, that I even have the ability to understand why it was that I was so enraged at the movie {Jurassic Park}.

I now know that it's God in me cringing at the very thought and the un-thankfulness of man failing to appreciate the fact that God gave the dominion; or the domination to mankind in the earth to conquer and to subdue the earth?

Those of which prefer curiosity over and against faith in God, they are missing out on the real true blessing of having dominion and the authority to conquer the earth. Curiously they are being led to follow a totally different path of life and of living on the earth. In all honesty and truth, many are looking for that to which they can never see and realize.

Curious minds as such, can not be settled to receive the word of God as the truth that it indeed is! As many look inside of the bible and struggle to grasp the mysteries of the gospel of God, curious others look away and on the outside of the bible for answers and or disapproval of the scriptural accounts, written therein.

Five

"Superstitious and Skeptical"

Superstitious ~ mythical, irrational, illusory, groundless, unfounded, unprovable, traditional - a belief or practice resulting from ignorance, fear of the unknown, trust in magic or chance, or a false conception of causation.

Skeptical ~ not easily convinced, having doubt or reservations, having an attitude of doubt, dubious, incredulous, mistrustful.

Then Paul stood in the midst of Mar's hill and said, Ye men of Athens, I perceive that in all things ye are too superstitious. For as I passed by, and beheld your devotions, I found an altar with this inscription, TO THE UNKNOWN GOD. Whom therefore ye ignorantly worship, him declare I unto you God that made the world and all things therein, seeing that he is Lord of heaven and earth, dwelleth not in temples made with hands. Neither is worshipped with men's hands, as though he needed anything, seeing he giveth to all life, and breath and all things.   Acts 17:-25;

Too Apprehensive to Protect the Things That You Trust In The Lord!

Apprehension is the fear of failing or of going forward. So many who are purported to be of the fellowship of the faithful, are not assured to the point of being empowered to move about their lives applying faith to every facet of their lives. They are now in the position of their lives whereas they are asking the questions, where do I go from here, and how do I go about living this new life in Christ?

They have been allowed to walk away from the altar of the churches, thinking that the salvation to which they had just believed to receive, may not be powerful enough to eradicate the power that sin had over their lives! Many who might have met them at the altar of the churches are yet just as superstitious and as skeptical as they are themselves.

Then on the other hand they spend too much of their time in the midst of truly faithless people! Even before leaving the churches many are congratulated for coming to the Lord to be saved, but only to say to them not to worry about doing things any differently, they are now secured as they live as they are pleased to do so.

Many think that they are successfully believing members of the churches now that they have been saved, who are simultaneously members of the doubtful superstitious skeptics of the secular society.

They are people who have come to the local churches, but they have not been born again into the fellowship of the church through the shed blood of Christ Jesus; having been wash through the word of God, and filled with the Holy Ghost.

As they walked the aisles of the churches to embrace the altar of God, many of the people never minded reciting a simple confession from their mouths. They feared being touched and totally cleansed from the inside out, and then filled with God's spirit. The Holy Ghost is God's spirit!

Although they walked the aisles during the call to discipleship, for salvation, skeptically many came forth saying; God if you're really real, come into my heart? Only their intentions of God moving into their lives is adamantly intended to be only an addendum to their way of thinking daily.

They like the idea of being able to say that they are a member of the church now. However, having God infiltrate their closets where superstition and skepticism is kept in secret is thought to be off limits, even to God! Superstitiously, many have been taught to believe that should they become too close to God, they will die!

We will all die when the time is appointed for our death. Superstitious and skeptics had gotten it twisted! The sinful nature of man, which brought about the curse of death on all of humanity, will have death reversed back onto it, and it will die. The power of sin over your life is what will indeed be reckoned as dead.

Multiples of people are in the local churches weekly and sometimes daily for services of many different types. For a truth, while it is that very many people are yet going to the churches consistently, they are not all growing in the way of the Lord. I have always observed the stagnant growth of the churches worldwide. I've been interested in knowing why this was so?

I've been guilty of living and behaving just like the people of the churches being a churchman my self. We dress in our finest clothes, and put on our most expensive cologne and leave our homes on our way to go to church. Only I realized the majority of my neighbors never left their houses to go out to attend a worship service on the Lord's day.

Not only did they not leave their houses to go to church, but on most occasions we never stopped to invite them to attend service with us. Figuratively speaking, the churches should have no walls, as result of bulging outwards from the people in attendance. Then of course the real question is; what is it about the people of the churches, that doesn't magnetize the sinners who are in need of being saved, pulling them into the churches to meet Jesus Christ?

I have found that the churches are filled with people that attend the services, that are otherwise broken, incompetent witnesses whenever they leave the sanctuaries. Most people take nothing with them biblically and spiritually to aid them as witnesses to the Lord. They are to the likes of people going on fishing trips, with no tools or bait for catching the fish.

Others might have been equipped with fishing rods, bait, nets and all other necessary tools for preserving the catch. However, the may not all be informed to know how to use the tools that they have! They attend Sunday School, and many other services where they hear sermons and messages from the written word of God. But, they are too often still in need of being informed of how to share the word of God in which they have received!

They might have received the letter, but they are lacking a higher level in the holy spirit to be enabled to maintain the attractiveness of the word to those that can and will hear the word and receive it, and the wisdom to know the difference in those who are not going to receive it from them.

Many of the services do not reach the purpose and or the level of what is to be only the true worship of God! Being that so many who come into the churches are superstitious and skeptical of the spirit of the Lord. We can never underestimate the fact that people's minds and their spirits are twisted and turned in many different directions, relative to receiving the truth.

You cannot question the truth of the Lord and worship Him all at the very same time. There has to be a delivery of the word of God through the spirit powerful enough to penetrate the rough exterior to enter into the mind and the heart of them that are the hearers.

The things of which we possess in this life must be covered by and through faith. Skepticism and doubt are assassins of faith! Faith is destroyed and obliterated in the presence of such negative elements. We need faith so desperately, we can't afford to allow ourselves to be skeptics and questionable, as individuals.

One of the greater plights of mankind, is the struggle of defining oneself! Someone has to assist us in our journeys to get to the foundational platform to discover who we really are and of where it is that we've come from. And even better yet we need to be directed into the right direction through the word of God, to be informed of where we are headed, as a result of receiving the Lord Jesus Christ into our lives.

Superstition and skepticism breeds fear and distrust! It's really not good to know that we need the help of someone who could really help us, but to be too uncertain about allowing their assistance to help us. You know, their knocking at your door, while you're afraid of opening the door to invite them in. I know the feeling of preaching and or teaching to an audience of people gathered at the church, who were questioning every word that was flowing from my mouth. The atmosphere was extremely tight and unreceiving.

How many times has there been occasions that you might have been given a wrapped gift where you might have struggled to even unwrap the package? Maybe it wasn't the gift itself; your skepticism was centered around the occasion.

You're basking in all sorts of questions about the meaning of the holiday. Perhaps you have began to question your beliefs? More often than not, you're not sure that you trust the person who gave you the gift. Only to name a few... Such is the very same as sharing the gospel of Christ Jesus, to a group of people that are questioning the reality and the truth of our Lord.

Supernatural vs. Superstitious

That which is supernaturally given to us from the spirit of the invisible God, through the written word of the scriptures-versus-that which is applied to us by a make believe source and sometimes from science. Though fictitious, it is also from a never realistically invisible host of unfounded thought, introduced to humanity.

The manifested help given to and supplied for the need of people far above and beyond the human ability to have those things is respectfully known as the supernatural. Of course the very formidable prefix to be recognized here is the prefix, the word "SUPER".

The extraordinary workings of the spiritual realm of which is associative to the reality of God the Father and the Creator of the world; of Heaven and Earth, is to be recognized as the supernatural. Deceptively though, many people in our world live every day thinking that they successfully ignore the reality and the truth of God.

Although all around the realm of humanity, it is known that God is The invisible God! Some people have taken it upon themselves to supply natural forms to call it god, or to suggest that it is god! The realistic truthful need for God, outweigh superstitious imagination. In the time of need there is no space or time for a fake or make believe substance to be the solution for a real problem. Problems that cannot be solved by our own human ability. Whenever we reach up for the higher power, the greater source ought to indeed be God that we are reaching up to!

Television programing and the movie industry has been quite instrumental aiding us with superstitious characters to embrace. Filling the emptiness in the otherwise necessary atmospheres, with immaterial hopelessness for the sake of entertainment. The creators of the fictitious characters know for sure that they are non-existent, but because of the vast majority of viewers, they have successfully continued to create mind boggling films.

It has been thought to be beneficial for the human mind to imagine the unimaginable, giving the space of thought in your minds to bring to life that which is indeed fictitiously unreal. You know for sure of the make believe characters to the likes of Superman, Mighty Mouse, Batman, Spider-man, Wonder Woman and God knows there are so many others.

Many have already been spiritually decapitated as result reading and studying Greek Mythology and Poetry, along with many other types of literature that doesn't at all faithfully stimulate the readers. Many mythological characters and creatures are used in comparison to Christ Jesus in many of the pulpits during a sermonic delivery.

Those characters are most passionately discussed than the savior who is real and alive right now! Theologians go on for a while admonishing the parishioners to give serious consideration to the mythological beings who're not even realistic. Some have thought it more befitting to refer to "The Beauty and The Beast" as a lesson of love in the churches over and against the word of God. Love Is God!

The psi-fi thriller films, which have generated the much

greater box office revenue income, have had an even greater grasp on the minds of people. Superstitiously, many would look to those fictitious characters in the times of need, rather than to look to the Lord Jesus Christ who is indeed real and truth.

Many people consider themselves to be a Trekkie, based of the Star Trek movie series. Amazingly in many of the big cities downtown, there are people dressed in the costumes of the super hero of their choosing. They can be seen wearing those costumes even when the temperature is soaring in triple digits.

Then there are the Star Wars movies and the characters that just will not be released from the thought processes of many people. People cringe whenever we might say to them; God bless you, or have a blessed day. But they grin and applaud when they hear someone say to them, may the force be with you. Many much rather believe in a force that they are not even aware of what it is! They flee and split the scene whenever they hear a mention of the spirit of God!

There may even be scientist in the laboratories attempting to bring dinosaurs back into existence. Jurassic Park lives in the minds of the superstitious. There just might be those people who are thinking that they would be interested in having a dinosaur for a pet, like Fred Flintstone. They might be thinking of bringing the stone age back?

They regard nature and the natural exo-spiritual realm, relative to that which is recognized as exoteric, as being the inexplicable reasoning for the human experience of living and of life in the earth. Having such freedom of thought and thinking, superstitious people are deceived, believing that they can reach into the outer realms of thought to create the source of their needs.

Nothing concrete would ever be found as the foundational platform for superstition that could result in what is to be regarded as true and tangible in the natural realm, among humanity. Mathematics teaches us that nothing from nothing, leaves nothing! Superstition is nothing! How is it that any people would have the idea as an human being to start out with nothing to create something?

It's evident that some people have forgotten that it is God who started with nothing to create all that there is that we are blessed with today as we are alive in the earth. Many people prefer ignorance over and above knowledge that speaks to the dominion and to the power of God. Which is the authoritative excellence of the supernatural, of our world.

The deity of God is greater than any other spirit or power of the universe. So many things and elements point to the creator, that are so amazing. No human being on the face of this planet, or in outer-space, could have ever been responsible for creating things as they are today!

Let's consider the birds of all species and sizes. We recognize them as birds, as result of their make and the manner of their style of living. They have wings, they have very strong beaks, and natural ability of flight, like no other created being. The super ability of their natural make up and kind, is in their ability to catch the gust of the wind.

Birds are not sitting in a classroom learning how to use their wings as they take to the air. In comparison to many other created beings, the brains of birds are very tiny. Yet they prove that they know what to do with their wings and how to use their beaks to extract food from it's sources.

Of all of the things that a bird may not be able to do, we must be willing to acknowledge all that birds can do. Have you ever watched a bird build a nest? Nature is the hardware stores, where they acquire building materials to construct their nests. It's not the size of their brains, as much as it is the knowledge that's naturally ingrained into them.

While Hollywood, Universal Studios and any other psi-fi

movie production company, would have us acceptably embracing the depiction of hideous monsters, though they are only fictitious on the big screen and on the television, they are disfigured and totally unnatural. However, they are a reality in the minds and the spirits of many people.

Monsters are of the most disturbing and frightening thing in the stretch of any abnormal human imagination. Children are naturally terrified whereas they can't sleep at night! They also develop an unshakable since of fear, some greater than others, causing them to be afraid of almost everything in existence.

Responsible parents won't allow for their young children to watch horror films, or movies during the holidays which depict some type of monster. These types of images are not easily forgotten and erased from our minds. It is far beyond my comprehension, the rush that some people get from being scared and afraid.

Many people will go to a haunted house to get that rush of fear! They have been encouraged to explore the depths of fear, before they would ever think of going to the church, house of God, to lend the opening of their minds to the teachings of faith in God.

Scary people, eventually as they mature to be older, are often shunned and stereotypically categorized to belong to any group of people who are never courageous and impossible of taking helm as a leader. However those who show a since of fear, may at times be preferred over those who are strong and courageous. Scary people are prone to raise their children as being scary also.

Dr, Smith from the television series show, back in the sixties, and the seventies, talked real tough and strong! Only to show a greater lack of confidence and strength when confronted by an alien monster in outer space. "Lost in Space" had us thinking that we just might be eventually looking to outer-space, and into the spooky psychological Halloween for all that is to be veered as the true realm of realistic supernatural existence?

We are seeing the supernatural everyday of our lives. However, we are often encouraged to give recognition to the natural realm, suggesting that nature is the self existing power of of our world. It is too often preferred that we should embrace the supernatural only as fiction.

Many are taught to avoid looking beyond the natural realm, attempting to see and even to know that which is indeed invisible, as it relates to knowing that God is indeed invisible. It's the invisible which is responsible for the motion and movement of the natural. You don't see your mind, but it is your mind that you are told to substitute and to put in place to tell you what to do and how to go about doing things.

Super ~ above, over or beyond......

Then there are the applied systems of behavior and of questioning everything. Whereas the applied systems are more so in place to supply another option rather than to accept and to believe that which has been established by God, is better referred to as superstition.

I like to think of superstition as to that of the methodology of a woven fabric. There are no fabric nor garments known to us in the earth that have not been stitched together in one fashion or another! No matter of how fine the fabrics and the fashionable attire are to us, human application has to be applied in an effort for the garment to have been put together.

Super-stitching, is what we are dealing with in the spiritual realm in an effort to bring the negative reality, and fear of the unknown element of superstition into fruition. It is not at all real! No matter of how you might have vigorously convinced your own mind to believe in the unbelievable, it's yet not real!

Growing up in school, we had a saying to any of our classmates, or to anyone in the neighborhood who had said something to us or about us that wasn't accurate or even true, we'd

say; "You Made That Up!" This is indeed what I'd say to many skeptics and to the superstitious, you made that up! You have woven that together on the table of your own imagination.

Your own mind have led you astray, to believe in something from outer-space! Whether it to be understood as being common or even uncommon to think way out, and far away as a method of dealing with daily affairs, it is indeed unnatural and unacceptable to the word and to the will of God for all humanity.

Through the power of the supernatural we are empowered to do things that our humanness is incapable of doing. Everything that is from God, is also likewise backed by the spirit, the power, and the word of God! God doesn't give humanity anything and leave us to handle it, or to make it work for us all of our own ability. That which is from God is designed to fulfill a divine purpose. The working power of the thing given to man is already fashioned and ordained to finish the assignment.

As human beings, we just need to be surrendered to God, the giver of all things supernatural by and through faith, and the applied success will be imputed to our will to complete the task given to us. In the realm of the supernatural we will not be found manipulating things so that they work for us. Much rather, supernatural things work in and through us to bring the required things in the spirit realm to pass.

Superstition and skepticism, lends to any people the reasons thought to be necessary never to trust in God. Therefore, many people will find themselves repetitiously chanting vain powerless words of evil origins, to acquire things in the natural realm of humanity that might have appeared to manifest outside of the natural realm. People are supplied the unreasonable platforms to avoid prayer and praying in faith to God. They'd rather pray to the elements of the sky, to the highest mountains, to one of the planets, or even to Satan.

In some way or another, the skeptics are deeply persuaded to avoid any such interactivity to the supernatural realm of the spirit of God! Many have behaved themselves so wildly and rashly, they are afraid that to come into the presence of God, thinking that it could mean immediate judgment and the sentencing of death for them!

These types of mindsets, suggest a total; disregard to the established written word of God, in the scripture of the Holy Bible! {King James Bible...}

The Skeptical Skip Over Real Truth

One of the more dangerous positions that people of the churches put most skeptics in is to agree with them! Suggesting that they see and that they may even understand what it is that they are conveying. Or, I know how you may be feeling about that. Or to suggest to them that they just may be right and correct about their ideas about the church and about God.

You, as a witness for the Lord, you are required to at least have an answer from the word of God, which speaks to their unreasonable spirit of doubt.

In not supplying them an answer from the word of God, you are assisting them with their lack of faith that is so necessary for every sinner to be saved. You as a churchmen are enabling the skeptics to exist like a floating bubble among the faithful people of God. But all of the while they are in need of having their negatively inflated bubble of an ego, to burst!

Perhaps you would take on a different position in your own Christian behavior and demeanor, if you were made aware of the fact that you are partnered with Satan, in keeping them on the fence! Or at the very most, in their determination to remain midriff, refusing to choose, they are enabled by a would be believer, to be on the outside of the reality of faith in God.

People must believe that "God;" is really who He Is! Before they are ever going to be able to enter into His presence and be glad about it.

Six

"Missed Them; With The Truth!"

Ever learning never able to come to the knowledge of the truth. II Timothy 3:7 ~ KJB...

"Aiming Right; But, Still Missing"

We; who are the ambassadors in the fivefold ministries of the Kingdom of God; we are indeed the called and chosen leaders according to the Purpose of the Lord. It is our assignment to give the truth of the written word of God; to the people of this world.

We study to rightly divide the truth, so as to have the people to see where the truth is to be applied to certain areas of their lives that need it. It is our desire that even the simplest of understanding, can get the message clear and void of any confusion.

We spend years, months, days and hours pouring over the same scriptures for the sake of knowing that we are not in error to what the spirit is saying to the churches.

As individuals of the clergy, it is likewise as important that we also live according to the truth that had been applied to our listeners.

As we determine to disciple the people of the churches it is even most necessary that we do not send cross messages of entitlement and of exclusion for those of us who teach.

My mother used to say to us back in our youth; what's good for the goose is also good for the gander. If it is good enough to give, it is also just as good to receive it as well!

In other words; she was not going to teach us to do things that she didn't think was also good for she and our father to do as well. Better yet, they were even more determined to teach and to lead us by their examples of living before us.

Now being a father myself, I have come to know that I am not the only influence that my children would ever have; to be honest my parents were not my only influences either.

This observation has been quite pertinent to the process of moving forward as a minister of the gospel of the Kingdom of God.

So as the people come into the churches to be saved and to adjoin themselves to the fellowship of the body of believers, it is going to be realized very soon that our messages are not the only message that they are going to listen to. Our voices are not the only voices that they are going to hear and give attention to.

It is very easy to be discouraged as a leader, when we know that we have studied to the point of even missing out on meals and praying for hours on end, seeking the Lord to give us the assurance that the truth that we have imparted to the attending crowd is accurate and scripturally sound.

As result, of watching a larger percentage of the people in the churches who fail to live the lives that we are teaching them to live, as they leave the church to go back to their lives in the society and the community.

So, in a since to go out of our way with the people in mind as we dig deeply into the written word of God and in the spirit; to be forced to face the fact that we had evidently missed the mentality of the people to adhere to the teaching of the word of God;

It's bad enough that now day's people are not nearly as attentive to the delivery of the messages as they used to be. It is most necessary at times to help ourselves out preventing the painful intrusion of guilt and of stress and anxiety not only in the churches but also in the world.

To those of us who really do care and are adamant about teaching and preaching a message that will change the lives of them that are attentive to messages is devastating and quite stressful!

I entertain the idea that the people of the churches should be probed from time to time so that as the leaders we can be made aware what they have actually learned and will have taken into their spirits and into their minds to actually apply to their lives on a daily basis.

I'm sure that the numbers would be astounding, as well as, disappointing? Everyone is not listening and paying attention to the messages in the churches, some simply are not yet on the comprehensive levels of understanding what is actually being taught.

Many people who attend the local church services, are yet quite curious about living according to the fashions of the world. It can be very difficult to indoctrinate the people of the churches who have never even brought their minds inside of the sanctuary with them (figuratively speaking), as a result of their curiosity of the things of the world.

No doubt about it, the people in the sanctuary are hearing what we say but they are a bit hindered as it might relate to listening to our instruction with the intent to obey what we have taught them.

It's not possible to put into practical application that which had been taught when you could never even comprehend the message! Far too many of the ministers are also curious and much less spirit filled!

So, what is more awe striking to them, is how well the house responds to the delivery of their spoken messages, knowing that they have failed themselves as it relates to being disconnected to the spirit of God; as a messenger of the gospel of truth.

Curiosity doesn't have the ability to allow for the heart of the ministers to be concerned as to how their messages are being applied in the lives of the people at home in their houses.

They are just satisfied that the people yelled and ran around the church if they are even allowed to do so in that particular church, in response to what they were saying.

In many instances; I sort of fault the ministers for allowing such uninhibited levels of curiosity to fill the sanctuaries of their churches. Even though people are who they are whenever they come into the churches, they are allowed to remain who they are as result of the lack of teaching and even more so of the lack of caring and failure to guide them as their leader.

Everyone in the church is not a con-artist or a scammer; those who are indeed, they will show you exactly who they are without putting forth much effort to do so!

Anointed ministers of God; should know to watch and to be prepared for such spirits and behavioral posture of the people sitting under their instruction.

However, in many of these situations we are dealing with ministers who have gone to higher learning institutions for the ministry, which never allowed for them to apply the spirit to the knowledge that they were gaining.

It is more likely that the spirit of arrogance and of pride will be allowed to saddle the flow of the messages in their churches.

Emerging as a prospective qualified minister to lead the people of the churches as a pastor, they are rather curious as to whether or not the information that they have received in school will work with the people who are in the churches?

They are already preoccupied with popularity and perception of the people, so much so that they have not even set their focus upon the spiritual need and the biblical awareness of the people.

The truth is that one element that must be established during childhood, else people have tendency to disregard as well as to disrespect the truth and them that tell the truth and carry it as a badge of honor.

Not a whole lot of people nowadays seriously interested in the naked truth, although we hear a lot jargon about transparency and being open to reality.

How to walk in truth as a child of the Kingdom of God and to discern truth in the lives of others is an ability associative to the knowledge that is gained through experience, as it is taught.

The greater perceptions are that people are preoccupied with whatever others think of them? In truth, they are otherwise poised to be the other individual that the others never even knew existed!

They are determined to master the costume and mask which covers their true identity. If they have anything to do with it you will never know that they have been acting and pretending all of the time.

Curiosity has set them on a platform to think of them as being winners, when in actuality, they have been on the failing decline, losing for a long time.

We come along reaching out to people only never realizing that they who we were determined to reach were never who we thought they were. Their stories about them changes every time that you talk with them?

They were always somebody else of whom we had never even met, simply because they were so excited to have been successful at deceiving other people.

The truth is that they are gloating over the fact that they tricked you into doing some things that you never would have even thought of doing, had you known the truth about who they really are!

So while they are feeling as if they have been successful at pulling off the scam, the truth is that we have missed them with the truth! They never allowed for us to find them and to reach them. Their curiosity is at a level too high for them to even settle down to be taught truth.

I believe that it is not their intention to reject the teaching and instruction of truth in the churches. Their conscience have been seared with a hot iron! To the point that their sensitivity has been shut down, whereas, they can't receive the truth in the word of God, in their heart.

Their senses have been dulled and shut off. They feel that the things on the outside of the churches and the bible, are much more satisfying and rewarding. They have been led to believe that the life of holiness and righteousness is a boring dull, uninteresting life to live! Little do they know!

"They'd Rather Hear the Negative Truth!"

The problem is that people of the churches go for the excitement and unfounded information that is interesting for common discussion among people who feel that they are all on common grounds.

As it relates to the truth, many people who are willfully disobedient to the truth of the written word of God; they often know that they are inadequate to handle the truth, being people who have rejected the truth themselves?

It doesn't stop quite a number of them from touching the things of God in the churches. They take the chance of altering the truth of the word anyway. They appear to have no fear of the Lord at all, as they go on forward in total error to the word and to the spirit of the Lord, all over the churches worldwide.

The erroneous ways of the leadership are supported all over the land. As there are more people who have adjoined themselves to the ways of the world and to demonic doctrines of the devil.

They know what the bible says; most of them anyway? But, they are determined to be identifiable to the systems of the society. They don't want to be shunned and rejected as most people who are righteously postured in holiness and truth are shunned and disdained.

So they have gone out of their way to soften the powerful blow of the word of God! When they deliver their messages to the churches; not realizing that what they have decided to bring to the people, is no longer even the truth of the bible.

Many of these leaders, are willing to cause separation and to maintain the breech with their family members, citing that people just don't understand?

It is suggested that the average people of the churches don't have the ability to understand the written word of God, since they have not attended any theological seminaries?

Such ideas about the people are used as a cushion for their determinate drive to handle the word of truth in error!

It is easily observed, as the people run swiftly to partake of the teachings that have been rung out and drained of the truth. Those who are taught intentionally wrong are the very same people who are advocates of their churches, and of their leadership!

People are led wrong daily, simply because they refuse to read the word of God for themselves. After reading, many of the people never find it necessary to seek the Lord for clearer understanding, they are satisfied with what they have been told at the churches.

A very painful reality is that they will be reminded how that they avoided the truth for a more comfortable negative spin on the truth! That was more agreeable to their own sinful lifestyle. More frequently now, people are not afraid to take a chance on dying in outright, out loud, sin and shame.

They have been allowed to believe that God intend for them to at least sin, lightly? Every sin, is going to net the sinner who actively lives and participates in sin, a sentence to eternal hell. Amen!

A demonic since of curiosity have hit the people of the church as of late! Whereas, certain people are thinking that they won't be able to go to heaven, so they are just preparing themselves to be in hell with their friends and their unsaved family members, that refused to obey the gospel of the Kingdom of God.

People that attend the churches now believe the messages of Hip Hop and secular influences, that suggest that there

will be the biggest party ever in hell; regardless of what the written word of God says about hell.

As we sit in the churches nowadays, and scan the faces of the people in attendance while the truth is preached, it doesn't take a rocket science, based on the facial expressions, to know who disapproves of the truth being spoken.

It is indeed curiosity that has failed the people, as they have received what they had never expected. They feel that just because they were indeed grown enough to go after what interest them, the churches should love them enough to mind its own business, and just let them be!

In other words, people prefer to be sinners and ungodly regardless to what the church is preaching and admonishing according to the scripture. How many times have you ever heard a sinner say to the people of the churches that; "I'm just as saved as you are?"

They feel that if they are able to spot the life of the saved people of the churches, that gives them the right to remain the sinner that they are?

The real truth is, there is nobody saved that never wanted nor intended to be saved! Regardless of the relationship that we have with the Father in Heaven, the people of the world and many in the churches, still refer to it all as religion.

People who argue and fight for the equal right to be in the churches, as a member of the local congregations, they out right refuse to be the church, according to the word of God.

They have the nerve to open their mouths as a witness, but are often devastated and confused when the people that they so-called witness to, rejects them.

People need to know, that although you are curious about salvation or at least about church, that doesn't constitute the fact that you have indeed been saved. The bible never instructs us that we should ever add curiosity to faith or as an addendum to salvation.

Curiosity never helps you as you purport to believe in God, and confess to be saved through repentance and faith in God; through the redemptive work of the cross at Calvary.

Suppose "Jesus Christ" had only been curious to see if we could make it back to the atonement with the Father in Heaven?

People are in the churches high fiving each other, for having suffered the consequences for doing the wrong types of things. They feel better connected to one another, knowing that they had each indulged into many of the forbidden things of the scripture.

The more negative detail an individual might have to report as a testimony, the more it is felt and believed by many of the listeners to be of an authentic accurate report.

Those who come forth reporting the truth, or reportedly too much of the truth for some people, they are considered to be rather crazy or too brave for haven divulged that information to the people of the churches.

I have to admit that they are not too far off from the truth about that, as many people of the churches are not really celebratory of other people's testimony! As they are curious to get out of church service to go and to Google, and to do research about that individual.

It is heartbreaking that so many people of the churches are

not willing to believe the testimony of another individual. They would much rather believe that those who confess to being saved and sanctified, and washed in the blood of Jesus Christ; that they could never be through with a life of willfully sinning.

As a matter of the fact, they are more adamant that it is not even possible to be finished with sin! Because so much sin is in the world. They can't seem to wrap their minds around the idea of not being sinful. Characteristics of the people who are in the world, is sinful, not godly.

I have even spoken with some ministers after a certain individual had given a testimony about their life from the past; I said to them that I was rather proud to hear that that individual had turned their life over to the Lord.

The pastor's response to me was that he didn't really believe that they had actually told the truth during their testimony. "Nobody is living that clean because you can't live free from sin; people don't live above sin!

He purposefully denied the truth that all people can be delivered from a life of willfully living in sin. Although the scripture admonishes us not to sin; I hear many of the clergy telling the people that now since they are saved, that God doesn't even see their sins as sins anymore!

What a lie from hell! It is this kind of message over the pulpit that the people are running to because of the fact that it caters to the lifestyle that they desire to live, in spite of the written word of God.

The truth is that most people have discovered that we cannot live free from sin on our own! However, it breaks my heart to hear them totally disregard the fact that Jesus died and rose to empower us to walk away from sinning willfully in our bodies, as a way of life.

The people of the churches have excuses simply because the clergy supplies excuses for them in their messages every Sunday morning.

The scripture admonishes us that; "we can do all things through Christ which strengthens us;" [Philippians 4:13] However, many of the ministers in their determination to make friends of the people of their churches, they are consistently telling the people; "I know that you can't help it; you can't do it; don't even worry about trying to do it; you might as well just go ahead and live as best as you can!

God knows your heart; He knows that you really wanted to live right?" Sin is only missing the mark; we all miss the mark every now and then, once a day or a little more? Being human beings, we just can't help but to sin. Real Lies; straight from Hell, the devil, and from the demonic influenced ministers in the pulpits, is what these are.

Far too many people are going into their graves daily, having lived as they were pleased to live, according to this type of teaching and ideas of living on a daily basis from the leadership in their churches.

They would much rather believe within themselves that they had trusted themselves to follow after leadership that believes in keeping it real! Somehow, they have allowed themselves to believe that the word of the bible and biblical teaching couldn't possibly be real?

I have spoken with too many preachers who were determined to show me that all of the preachers and the members in their churches were all guilty of living a life riddle with sin and iniquity, still!

The suggestion to me was that I was teaching the people in the church that I pastored, way too much? It was said to me that the people didn't need to know that much information about the bible and about living holy.

I went to help a friend with his church; his messages were consistently filled with the fleshly behavior and the good times of the club from the past. His simple admonishment was that the people needed to come to the church at the certain times of the week and on Sundays; now that they are saved.

He talked about being a playboy; and a real cool dancer on the floor at the club. He talked about how he had it going on, and of how well liked he was as a person?

Having been a member of the church for all of his natural life, seems to me that he should have been more biblical prepared to share the message of the gospel of God.

He opened his bible indeed to share the message to the church, but after reading the scripture there was not really much that he had to say on the scripture.

His level of curiosity was to see how many people really identified with the life that he had from the past! So he went on for a while from the pulpit bragging about him, leaving very little space for the truth of the word of God.

We were never called of God; to forget about God in the pulpit while we preach to the people of the churches.

"On The Other Hand;"

While all of these masters of deception and lies seem to have the churches going with their deceptive mannerisms and behavior, they think that they are sure that we of the churches won't see them for who they really are?

Sadly, the truth is that the ministry of the churches have too often missed those very needing individuals during the opportunities to share nothing but the truth to them as they attend the services at the churches!

Many expository preachers are huffing and puffing, rhythm and rhyming, arguing and debating hypothetical issues in the pulpits. They have learned to have theological sermonic discussions right int he midst of their sermons, but they are arguing with other Theologians who are not even present to hear their debates?

All along the time of their delivery, many of the people are lost and bewildered, they have even mentally dismissed themselves, although they are there in attendance, by their own will.

Many people are encouraged to take their time getting to know the Lord, very slowly! Often they are admonished not to get in a hurry, or even try to get too deeply into the knowledge of the Lord? Like they really need to go that slow?

Respectfully, they are not considering that time is not at their disposal. We live by the gift of time, but that doesn't mean that time is our own personal friend. Time shouldn't be what we depend on. Time is not promised to us!

Time may stop for us and leave us behind at any uncertain moment! Time continues to move on forward ticking away

at each second towards the coming of the Lord, as people continue to live! While living for many other people will have ceased.

The people of the churches are actually much more gullible to receive whatever has been said. They are curiously negative about the actual messages from the bible.

Even though the man or woman will have said a certain thing over the pulpit during their sermonic delivery, most people are not going to search the scripture for themselves.

So in actuality, it is the preachers themselves as they are self-absorbed and egotistically bolstered to believe that they are the greatest deliverer of the message of the gospel, ever!

They pursue their own curiosities with all of the intellectual gravitational force that they can put forth. While they are adamant to ignore what needs to be said across the pulpit that will cause the people to be convicted of the sin in their lives.

Some people have even come into the churches to get an approval from the leadership to be more committed to finding themselves in the midst of their sins.

Often they have come into the churches expecting to hear messages that convict them, only to be disappointed with the message and the messenger.

Others; they go as far as wanting to know that we of the churches can see them in the exact state that they are in, whenever they came into the church. Dangerously they play along the religious lines of saying; "please be patient with me, God is not through with me yet!"

The truth is that they never intended to change from their

desired style of living sinfully, they needed to feel as if they had added a since of God to their own choice of living? They want the people of the churches and the leadership to know exactly who they are without a doubt!

We of the churches have the truth for sure, but what it is that we are lacking is the drive to kill the curiosity through the written word of God; as curious people enter into the fellowship of the churches.

Again, curious leaders would rather flirt with the idea of possibly being able to channel the curiosity that people are carrying on the inside of themselves for their own benefit.

As they battle the God complex as the leader, they are missing the fact that the people are daily being more and more affixed to a mentality which suggest to them that the leadership understands and supports sinful living from the people in the congregation.

Curiosity has been allowed to set the frequency of listening to the hell-bound calls of the abyss playing the songs titled; "Try Me!"

Until you really learn to love people and are determined to see them saved set free and delivered from the life of sin and shame, you couldn't possibly care that they are hindered and simultaneously driven to chase after the things of the world.

They come into the churches bearing that one element that will have them confessing Christ, while behaving themselves to fit into the clubs and gangs of the society that tell a much different story about them.

We speak of people being hypocrites in the churches but the reasons that we have not been successful at reaching

them to know why they are so hypocritical, is because we fail to discern the spirit of curiosity that is working within them.

People become what they really do hate and would otherwise despise, as a result of being curious about what they are looking at in the lives of others.

Without prayer on a consistent basis, proper teaching in the word of God; and the indwelling power of the Holy Ghost; what you focus on is what you will eventually become.

People backslide from the churches being so curious about the things that they had never tried and the people that they had never met, who are living in sin, having no desire to be saved and delivered.

They sit in the churches and observe while many preach the truth to people who are so curious that they have caused train wrecks in the church. They have set fires among the people of the churches that should be otherwise peaceful and full of love for one another.

Many of the leaders will sit back and watch things blow up around the churches, while they are determined to just allow for the things to work themselves out. Only, by the time those things had finally settled, many people had been devastated and seriously bruised.

Some had walked away from God and not only just away from that church. They now have a bad taste in their spirit for anyone who confesses to being born again in Christ Jesus.

Curious leadership is more determined to see how the people come together; even though they are witnessing that they don't know how to do it. It doesn't make good sense for the leadership to turn a blind eye to the one who caused all of the ruckus and the stink in the church.

People are outraged when another person allows for their pet to go to the bathroom in their yard, without cleaning up the mess! So surely a sanctified leader should know that a mess can't be left to itself; as messes don't clean itself up!

Curious people that are allowed to stir up trouble and strife among the fellowship are soon going to launch an assault against the position of the leadership.

They also know what things would be like around the church had they been checked and put back into their rightful place as a respectful member of that church?

Consider the fact that certain people may only be acting out in the churches because they are curious to see how the leadership will respond to the trouble?

King Saul; was sent on a mission with a direct charge from the Lord; he failed to complete the assignment, as ordered of the Lord.

He came back to the camp in the city where they resided only to face the Prophet Samuel; he enquired of Saul; "have you done as the Lord your God had commanded you?" Saul was quick to answer the prophet saying;" "yes I have done as He asked for me to do."

The prophet says to him; "what is the bleating of the sheep that I hear, and the lowing of the cattle?" For and answer; Saul begins to levy the blame on the people who were following his leadership.

He said that the people saw that the spoils were good for sacrifice and offerings to the Lord. I can't appreciate how Saul took the Lord's command and turned it into something

that the Lord was never asking for him to do.

Studying the life and the times of Saul; it is obvious to me that he was quite a curious individual. Being as curious as he was, he always managed to do whatever he desired to do among the people, and before the Lord.

The last curious act of Saul; caused God to rend the Kingdom from him as King over all of Israel and Judah. His disobedience as result of his own curiosity was the demise of his own leadership as king, and the ruler of the people.

As curious as many of the leaders of today are, I wonder how it is that they have missed the truth of the word of God in how that the Lord does not delight in curious acts of ego and of pride.

God has left no secrets as to how He will judge them that disobey His word! There is no special favor given to the leaders who have their own ideas about how the things in the churches ought to be handled, regardless to the leading of the spirit and the written instruction in the bible.

The question in my own mind is how do such curious leaders even lay down to sleep knowing that they have intentionally disregarded the word of the Lord concerning the people of His Kingdom?

The definition of leadership is not; "stand at the front and be the one that everybody see as the person in charge?"

Even though you decide not to put your shoulder to the wheel, so to speak; you have been called to set in order, the established direction that the Lord had already required for the people of the churches; the children of faith in God to go in.

Leader; you are to see to it that the people of God are all about the Father's business in the churches. As leaders it is our position to teach the people of the churches to know when they have indeed learned to please the Lord, both in what they say and do!

It is most discouraging to have to teach and then to have to reteach the very same messages in the bible, but only because the people had never been able to grasp the teaching of truth. But a dedicated leader will surrender to the need of the people and teach it anyway.

A parent doesn't stop giving medicine to their child because the first dosage didn't cure the cough! The medication is administered as often as it is needed until the cough has been cured.

When a shepherd has ministered to the flock only to discover that they are still in need of being fed; if they are indeed giving and loving shepherds, they will again feed the flock.

A very sorry and defeated attitude of a shepherding leader of the churches of God, is to say of the people in the churches that they just ought to know what to do and how to get it done to please the Lord?

As leaders we are to be able to give account for the people that follow our leadership. But, what do we say for the people if we never teach them and give to them that which is required and expected of them when enquired of the Lord?

Perhaps the leaders failed to know that the blood is required at their hands. Yes, the people will answer to the Lord for the lives that they will have chosen to live.

Even when the leadership has been faithful to teach them to live righteously and holy unto the Lord, they will answer according to whether or not they obeyed the gospel of God.

Doesn't matter how unnecessary and foolish the people feel that preaching the gospel is to them, those who are called of God must continue to preach the word of God with power and conviction.

In all truth and fairness to the leadership; many of the people that we are missing with the truth of the gospel, we may never even know until in the judgment.

Many of the people that we might have even been sure that they had received our report of the Lord, were secretly curious about the kingdom of darkness and of all that is displeasing to the Lord.

Although we preached until our clothes dripped with sweat, and our bodies were drained of its energy, there were some people who were never going to be touch with the message.

"?~Too Many Teams To Play For~?"

Everybody wants to play for a winning team, but, too often the players that are seeking to join the team, are not even willing to put in the work required to be on the team. Many of the general team players despise practice! They believe that they are good enough to get on the playing field and to defeat any opponent.

Many people are overwhelmed with their own skillful ability to play the game according to the established rules. They are convinced that no one could ever play the game as well as they do. It is often not until they get on the field and get totally annihilated by the opponent that they even begin to realize, just how inflated their ego has been blown up and out of control!

The people in the churches get overwhelmed about the congregation and of the leading personality of that ministry. Although they are sooner or later found to be biblically abandoned on the side of the road, they are too embarrassed to acknowledge they had chosen the wrong team.

The leaders who preach the unadulterated truth of God's written word, are pitching hard balls, fast balls from the word of God, straight across the plate. Sadly, those who are indeed curious about everything, never prepare and set themselves for the skilled pitcher.

We live in a society that appear to have produced many batters who have struck out! They have never developed the skill to see the fast balls coming across the plate. They don't have the what it takes to hit home runs, and to score for the sake of a team win.

Sadly, but, too often we are truly missing the people with the truth of God, simply because the truth is really not what the people are seeking. People are in search of support from other people who are experiencing the same things as they are themselves.

The truth is that most people are not always looking to rid themselves of the pains and disappointments in their lives, as much as they are seeking to find other people that just may have found a method of dealing with all of it, without the aid of the written scripture? Even though they have come into the churches for solutions.

The truth is, not everyone that know how to do church, have a relationship with the Lord. To know churches of all types, according to their doctrines and methodologies is one thing, to know God is a totally different reality all together!

Just because a building may haver a steeple atop of the roof, doesn't mean that the truth of God in Christ Jesus; is taught and preached on the inside, without error! Lots of people know how to look and to act as if they have it all together, when in fact they are all jacked on the inside.

They have never given themselves to the Lord! They are dried out having never allowed the spirit of the Lord to fill them on the inside. The greatest error is to sit in the churches in the presence of preaching from the bible that you may not have ever intended to hear, and to receive! The only way to ever allow the word of God to follow you as you leave the fellowship of the church, is to let it into your heart, mind and your soul!

The word of God doesn't hitch a ride on your back as you leave the church, seeking a place to find rest and or a place of residence, to call it a home. You must open up and receive it, while you're in the midst of the message. The ball is in your court, it's your move!......

Seven

"Curious; But, Uninterested"

And when the Philistines heard the noise of the shout, they said, What meanest the noise of this great shout in the camp of the Hebrews? And they understood that the ark of the Lord was come into the camp. And the Philistines were afraid, for they said, God is come into the camp. And they said, Woe unto us! for there hath not been such a thing heretofore. And there ran a man of Benjamin out of the army, and came to Shiloh the same day with his clothes rent, and with earth upon his head. And when he came, lo, Eli sat upon a seat by the wayside watching:

FOR HIS HEART TREMBLED FOR THE ARK OF GOD. AND WHEN THE MAN CAME INTO THE CITY, AND TOLD IT, ALL THE CITY CRIED OUT. AND WHEN ELI HEARD THE NOISE OF THE CRYING, HE SAID, WHAT MEANETH THE NOISE OF THIS TUMULT? AND THE MAN CAME IN HASTILY, AND TOLD ELI. [1 SAMUEL 4:6-7; 12-14] AND WHEN SIMON SAW THAT THROUGH LAYING ON OF THE APOSTLES' HANDS THE HOLY GHOST WAS GIVEN, HE OFFERED THEM MONEY. SAYING, GIVE ME ALSO THIS POWER, THAT ON WHOMSOEVER I LAY MY HANDS, HE MAY RECEIVE THE HOLY GHOST. BUT PETER SAID UNTO HIM THY MONEY PERISH WITH THEE, BECAUSE THOU HAST THOUGHT THAT THE GIFT OF GOD MAY BE PURCHASED WITH MONEY. THOU HAST NEITHER PART NOR LOT IN THIS MATTER: FOR THY HEART IS NOT RIGHT IN THE SIGHT OF GOD. [ACTS 8:18-20]

"They Heard Them; Just as They Hear You Now!"

People are really curious to know things which makes them seen and respected as relevaznt among their peers. But most often is not at all that they desire getting intimate with the knowledge that they have acquired.

To be enhanced and or to be made relevant among the people who are indeed in the know, is not at all what they are desiring. They just want to be counted worthy to be compared as viable to challenge the leading people of the society, who are also known for being knowledgeble and well versed about a lot of societal issues!

We have seen for decades; for an instance when a

crime or an accident will have occurred, how that many people will come to see what happened, but upon being questioned they are not hesitant at all to let the authorities know that they don't want to get involved. But they wanted to know what happened?

As the over-blown levels of curiosity has hit the land these days, should trouble befall you in some way or another, you're in even bigger trouble than you might have ever thought possible for you.

Consider the fact that curiosity has caused a serious shift in what people care about and of how they choose to respond to what happens.

It used to be a time that if you got into trouble of some kind and other people were around they might be apt to get involved with you to help you. In this age of the cell phones, most people now days will pull out their phones and begin to record the ordeal, and begin to snap pictures.

They will take pictures, but not for your benefit; they are seeking to go viral on the web, brandishing their skills of photography! They are curious indeed, but not at all interested in helping you.

One of the most attracting tragedies to happen to people in the history of civilization had been for their homes to catch fire and burn. Curious people from miles away who could see the large plumage of smoke would come to see what was going on.

However, most of them would stand back off in the distance just close enough to see what was happening to your home.

But they dare not to get involved with trying to extinguish the blaze, because of fear and the eminant danger involved.

Should one of your loved ones die suddenly; or should they be missing and can't be found; many people will come around to find out what happened?

However, they're never intent on getting involved in the search to find them, or to assist with the final arrangements and support to bid them, farewell.

There may even be those people who are aware of what happened, although they may not be knowledgeable as to why it all happened; but they will adamantly refuse to get involved to say at least what it is that they know.

Let there be a conspiracy going in the churches about an individual, whether they are a leader or just a layman. Others who are indeed aware of the originator; and are aware of what is being said about a person; may never reveal that they knew all along.

While they entertained you, supposedly consoling you, helping you to get pass the secret scandal of the grapevine.

That person may walk about the churches with the individual of which the conspiracy is all about, but they will never divulge to anyone that they knew what was happening for the sake of bringing an end to the evil matter. But, they knew all along!

Often in a group of people at a crowded event,

someone's purse or wallet may be stolen. The person standing right next to the thief who saw everything, will remain tight lipped and allow for the thief to get away with the crime for a lack of interest in seeing a criminal brought to justice.

Mind you that they really have no problem with you; they have just been curious for some time in their own lives, to see such drama take place right before their eyes.

In that instance, they are curious to see just how long it might be that the culprit may escape being found out, so they will play the little game of acting as if they never saw anything.

Here in the scriptural account of the Israelites and the Philistines; out on the battlefield where the Israelites were taking a very bad beating in defeat of their enemy.

The Israelites came up with a strategy that they were sure would change the outcome of what was indeed taking place against them in the battle.

Now the Israelites were curious to see if they could rather move God to give them the victory over the enemy. However they failed to go about inquiring of the Lord in the proper manner already ascribed of the Lord.

The men of the Israelite army decided to go into the holy place to get the Ark of the Covenant of the Lord; of which they were never to even approach it, nor to handle it with their hands. Never being anointed to handle the Ark by God, who gave the covenant from the beginning.

Having the Ark of the Covenant with them

on the battlefield, they decided that they knew how to further help the Lord. They agreed among themselves to let out the noise of a great shout, as if their help had arrived!

The Philistines curiosity became aroused once again! They had been made familiar to the entrance of the presence of God; among His own people.

Their question was; "what is the meaning of this noise that the Israelites are making?"

Somehow, they were made aware that the Ark of God; that it had been brought into the camp with the Israelites.

To the Philistines this meant utter destruction for them! They were afraid, yet they were curious about the presence of the Lord; they thought anyway?

The Philistines were curious about the Ark of God; but they were uninterested in the Lord of the Israelites. Their decisions were to get over being afraid and to fight against the Israelites and their God; even though it meant their demise.

However, as the Philistines began to fight against Israel; they discovered that Israel had been even more curious than they had been.

There was nothing in the camp with them but their noise. The enemy had an even greater respect and knowledge of the Ark of the Covenant than to those of whom God had given it to.

This repetitive behavior of people stepping into the holy places of authority to do things, that they were never called and anointed to do, is occurring in the churches all across the land nowadays.

The Israelites were familiar to the noise of worshiping God; as it is reported that Joshua at the battle of Jericho; sent the armies of Judah out first for seven days to march around the walls of Jericho.

On the seventh day, they were to let out the biggest shout ever made of them. As they did do so, the walls of Jericho came tumbling down!

That's right, God; did it for them, through their praise and the noise of their shout. But where it is that many people get it wrong, they are determined to believe that it was just the noise that made the difference at that battle!

On the battlefield, even though the Israelites knew that it wasn't just the noise of the great shout, being curious as to whether or not the Philistines were knowledgeable of that fact, they thought to give it a shot anyway?

Whenever we of the churches go forth to make noise in the churches, it had better be known that God is in the midst of the noise!

MAKE A JOYFUL NOISE UNTO THE LORD ALL YE LANDS.
PSALMS 100:1

The psalmist here admonishes us to make a joyful noise; i.e. joy-filled noise! He never said nor intended to say to us; just make some noise; as we often hear today; "somebody make some noise in here!"

I am of the noisy crew who make a joyful noise unto the Lord during our worship services. But to those who know me, they can tell you that I am not an advocate, nor a supporter of just loud unspecified and unskillful, none melodic noise.

Unnecessary purposeless noise drives me up the wall and back down the other side! There is just no need for making a bunch of noise for no reason.

We serve a God who is seeking spiritual and truthful worshippers to worship Him in spirit and in truth. Many people have gotten it twisted in that they think that they are seeking the Lord while participating in making great noise in the sanctuary?

No; but rather, we are worshiping God because we already know that He is God; and that there is none other like Him. Worshippers are already acquainted with who God is!

We do not even worship God to bring Him into our presence; while we do enter into the presence of the Lord as we worship Him! I do believe that the Israelites thought they would bring the spirit of the Lord into the battle with them.

They soon discovered that they had deceived themselves; as they further took the beating on the battlefield that they would have never taken had the Lord been with them from the beginning of the battle.

People are pushed with curiosity to do that which the Lord had never called upon them to do in the churches. We live in a generation where people are most curious and determined to take the microphone.

Everybody wants to be heard speaking to the people of the churches over the microphone. They are curious to know what it feels like to be recognized as the person who spoke to the church.

There was a witness from the battle who came back to report what happened in the battle; as he began to tell the people what had indeed taken place on the battlefield.

The people began to also make great noise, but for the sake of the pains of losing the battle and the Ark of the Covenant!

I am mindful of the amusement parks; when driving bye, a passenger in an automobile might begin to express their curiosity about the park, wondering about the rides and sharing their excitement, wanting to know about all of the events and the attractions.

As result of hearing the noise of the rides and the excitement of the people as they partake and enjoy the rides and the games of the park, their curiosity grew more and more. Many of the parks have entertainment of all sorts going forth simultaneous to the regular attractions.

Once those who have been made curious make up in their minds to go and to see what the noise is all about; the tickets are purchased and the entrance to the park is made?

However the person who made all of the noise about going to see the attractions of the park for themselves, upon their entrance to the park they fearfully make the decision to be stationary around the front entrance of the gate never moving into the interior of the amusement park? They made a lot of noise and even convinced us that they were indeed curious about the park?

To our surprise, they were actually a bit more uninterested of seriously partaking in any of the exciting noise stirring attractions of the park! They just wanted to see what the noise was all about.

Have you ever been at the mall or in a department store with someone, and all they talked about was visiting a certain department store in the mall?

Walking through the mall bypassing all of the other department stores to honor the request of the other individual? Spending time looking around and examining several items closely, at that one chosen store?

The other shopper finds the items that they have been intrigued to have, we thought anyway?

Very soon it is clear to everyone else that they would like to have the item, but at an instance they are uninterested to complete the purchase!

They've had a change of heart about the item. They walk out of the store empty handed, though they had the money to buy what they wanted.

Sometimes people are curious about all of the noise that has been going around about a certain restaurant? They will make the decision to go and to see for themselves, what the noise is all about?

They walk inside and look over the menu, and inquire of the prices, stand there for a moment indecisive, turn and walk out of the restaurant without ever making a purchase.

We have been taught throughout the centuries that living is all about making choices. I can't but help to agree with this fact!

However, I have discovered that the multiples of colors and the magnitude in the decisiveness of our choices, is hinged upon the curiosity in our minds. That will often be the hindrance of the progression in our stride, to advance froward in the progression of our decisions.

Whether we will choose to indeed go with our curiosity, or to obey the writing of the scripture and deny ourselves is the difference that will determine the outcome in how it is that we determine to make the choices that are available to us.

"Pulling Away; While Being Drawn To the Spirit of The Lord; Simultaneously!"

Many people, who feel that they are indeed being pulled into the direction of salvation and deliverance, are pushing against surrendering to the will of the Lord.

I'm talking about the very same people who purposefully avoid going to the church but they are dedicated to showing up at the party and the club. They bear the sense of desiring to be saved and changed from the life they are living that is displeasing to the Lord.

They are aware that there is a greater life worth living that is designed for them, but the curiosity in their minds has a greater pull in interest than their desire to come on to the Lord.

They have the conversation going on in their heads and even in their hearts when they're all alone by themselves?

But, the very moment they come into contact with people who are indeed saved and filled with the Holy Ghost; the set themselves on the defensive to argue against the truth that is being shared with them.

Even though they know that it is the truth being brought to them by the word and of the spirit of God.

Faith; is greater than curiosity! Believing, alone all of itself, allows for curiosity to reside right along with what has been taught and believeed to be faith, in the heart and with the outlasndish thoughs and questions of the mind.

Curiosity can be allowed to be the possible second choice just in case the first choice of faith, so called; doesn't pan out for them?

However, faith my friend, it nails the very decisiveness of choosing, as to the likes of being the only choice which could be no other choice than God; in Christ Jesus!

Being left up to you and to me; having been chosen as the screening process for our choices, curiosity at its very best, bears the authority to only question whether or not we desire to see or to experience certain things in our lives?

But, it is void of the weight of gravity to produce what is truly desired of us.

However, faith is totally left up to God, all that is necessary for us to do, is to align ourselves with the written word of God. Rely upon faith in the word through prayer, in the name of Jesus; and God will do the best!

Curiosity demands that you look away from the word and the will of God. There is no way to simultaneously look to the Lord and to also likewise entertain curiosity. One will outweigh the other, causing you to choose.

A very real truth is that people want more of what the world might have to offer than they want from God.

As of late, the carnal minded people of the secular society and of the churches have joined together. Deciding that there should be the developement of a new society of the churches, which allow for the sinful behavior of the world and for the mandated lifestyle of the people of the churches, to mix as one reality!

As people continue to avoid the teachings of holiness and of righteousness, they become easy targets to be deceived and tricked into believing that they can now tell God what they want in the churches and then to have God to agree with them?

The written word of God is life and the thread of living in the natural bodies of the earth. That part of us that we know of and respect as being the flesh, is that part of humanity which separates us from the spirit of God, and true holiness and righteousness.

Curiosity; resides in the spirit of the flesh which drives us to want to know things and to have the control of things in the earth outside of God.

I know that I have said often what I will also say again; "people want God's stuff and all that He has to offer to us; but they don't want God!"

Even many of the people who have indeed been saved and washed in the blood, if giving the opportunity to be left to themselves while desiring the thing of the spirit of God; they become just like Simon the sorcerer?

Simon wanted the power to give other people the Holy Ghost by the laying on of his hands; but for an agenda of his own.

Note: Simon; himself, had not even been filled with the Holy Ghost! But, he though it appeared to be a very miraculous enough ordeal to desire that it be given to other people; probably for an hefty price?

He marveled at the power of the Holy Ghost, as anyone will that will have the opportunity to witness the working power in operation.

Only Simon's greater curiosity was all about being able to manipulate the power of the Holy Ghost, from his own perspective, imagining the influence that he could gain?

He was indeed curious about the Holy Ghost; be he had no interest in being filled with the Holy Ghost for himself.

Simon is exactly just like many people of today; they may not go out in the market and in the malls to try and sell the Holy Ghost to people that might want it. But somehow or another they have imagined a scheme for a financial gain as

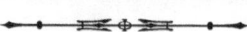

Curious, But Uninterested

result of the spirtual flow in their churches?

However, many are standing in the pulpits carrying on as the leaders, when it's all about the money.

Not only are they not interested in trying to get the people of their churches to be filled with the Holy Ghost; they don't allow for the Holy Ghost to even be at work in the sanctuary where they reside as the leader.

Simon knew that what the apostle's carried about in their spirit was from God. He just thought that he would try and get what they had by paying instead of praying!

So many people today have likewise been deceived and misled concerning what it requires to be filled with the spirit of the Lord.

They are faithfully paying for that that can only be acquired by praying and fasting. Tithing doesn't award you the Holy Ghost; you should never be a faithful tither and never be filled with the Holy Ghost.

The people of the churches today ignore a message as to this one, no matter what you say to them, their decision is to pay, and to disregard the need to pray!

The number of paid programs in the churches has increased tremendously, but there is still more people in attendance at the pay per view services than there is at a free-will prayer meeting.

People much rather pay than pray!

Those that are indeed curious, show up with their money, on the other hand those who are

interest in coming on the Lord side, they show up with their hearts and their whole selves before the Lord; surrendering and ready to receive Him.

> BUT AS MANY AS RECEIVED HIM, TO THEM GAVE HE POWER TO BECOME THE SONS OF GOD, EVEN TO THEM THAT BELIEVED ON HIS NAME. [ST. JOHN 1:12]

Many people will come to church with you at the drop of a hat, but don't expect for them to commit to your church just because they came. In many instances they are curious about what it is that has your interest at the church of your choice? But they have no desire to be there with you?

They can't seem to wrap their minds around your commitment to regularly attend weekly services. And they certainly can't get with the idea of giving their money in tithing, sowing seeds of faith, and giving freewill offerings every time that they show up to the church?

They have a great sense of curiosity, but curiosity is not faith and you my friend, ought to know the difference having the spirit of discernment working in you.

So many people that you might feel that you are witnessing to, as they give an ear to hear your conversation, they are only curious as to what it is that you will actually say that you believe?

The people who themselves are interested in the Lord are also likewise interested in the word of the Lord. You will find that they are readers of their own bibles just as you are.

You see, people do find their way to the Lord having had no desire to do so! An interest in the Lord starts the drive on the inside of your spirit soul and your body to make a move to get in the direction of searching and finding God.

Even the Holy Ghost; is only given to believers who ask for it; else everyone would be walking around with the power of God flowing out of them.

"Inquiry Minds Get Busy With Your Business!"

> FOR WE HEAR THAT THERE ARE SOME WHICH WALK AMONG YOU DISORDERLY, WORKING NOT AT ALL, BUT ARE BUSYBODIES. AND WITHAL THEY LEARN TO BE IDLE, WANDERING ABOUT FROM HOUSE TO HOUSE; AND NOT ONLY IDLE, BUT TATTLERS AND BUSYBODIES, SPEAKING THINGS WHICH THEY OUGHT NOT. BUT LET NONE OF YOU SUFFER AS A MURDERER, OR AS A THIEF, OR AS AN EVIL DOER, OR AS A BUSYBODY IN OTHER MEN'S MATTERS. [II THESSALONIAN 3:11; 1 TIMOTHY 5:13; 1 PETER 5:15;]

Everywhere you go, people want to know, all that there is to know, but for no other reason than to be tagged as one who has got the scoop on all of your business, and the details of your most private affairs.

Not to the likes of attending college for many years acquiring several degrees for the benefit of career opportunities and financial gain. They desire rather to know just because they want to be the eyes and the ears of the neighborhood and the community.

Such people are never bolstering their knowledge base for the benefit of you. Even though it is your business and all that concerns you that they are digging and turning over things to get information about you.

We have always referred to them as nosy busybodies and people that snoop in other folks business. They are the kinds of people that have reported on you, spreading information on you, that you are not even aware of.

I have been confronted by people that I have never even personally talked to myself! Who were sure that knew exactly what I had done? Who I did it with? How much money that we spent wherever we went and so on?

God only knows the times that I had been approached by pastors, bishops and other people of the churches. They were set on telling me that they had been informed of who I am?

As it relates to the scandal around the churches, those who are the leaders will have the information of the scandal, haven never even spoken with the individual of which all of the noise is about.

The person they are talking to, doesn't stand the chance of being able to tell the story for them. They have been made aware of some stuff, mainly because they desired to know. Now they are sure that they know you better than you!

People, who watch you and never see the behavior or the characteristics of the repot on you, still will not let go of what they have been told about you. Perhaps they have desired to know some things about you for a very long time? Curiosity will have you believing in the wrong sources?

There is a difference when certain knowledge has been brought to you, and when you are one who chased after the knowledge of certain people.

There is a society around the churches of whom we had dubbed them as the church Mafia; being that they are so curiously inquisitive about other people in the churches and downright inclined to know all of the knowledge that they can get about other people.

Certain people we outright refused to fellowship or to be relaxed around them, cautious as to whether or not we would be their very next target! That is of course, if we had not already become the target of their inquiry minds.

Being taught accountability in the churches, we were taught to say; "if you see me walking, and I'm not walking right; say a prayer for me and show me where I may be wrong?"

But I can tell you that there have been people in the churches who never gave you a chance to be out of order. They have no problem at all creating a scenario or spreading a rumor truly unfounded!

Many of the curious leaders will know of such a situation and they may even be made aware of the pain that it might have caused you. Their admonition to you is to "get over it!"

They may call you in to check you about the rumor, but they will almost never check the individual who brought the rumor to them. All too often the busybody is awarded and given outright

support over the pulpit.

Doesn't matter how you might secretly report on another individual, you can't make them to live holy through the fear of being reported on or exposed. The sickening games that are played with the lives of the people of in the churches must be put to a stop.

Alike the Israelites (the church folk); who were on the battlefield in a war who took that Ark of the Covenant; where it was never to have been taken; people need to stop trying to help God!

For the lack of better words or for the fact that we really didn't know what to call it; we had donned those people as being messy! They cause a great big mess many times on the strength of their own curiosity. How is the pastor going to deal with this one?

I wonder if they are going to stay with this church now when all of the stuff comes out? How are they going to respond knowing that I told on them?

It's all a game that the busybodies play among the people of the churches. There is nothing genuine, about being genuinely curious?

There is no way to say that you were seriously concerned about the other individual; other than just to go ahead and to lie! It's time that we of the leadership learn to take authority and pray earnestly that the spirit of curiosity can be put out of the conversations and the matter that belongs to the Kingdom of God.

Salvation places a greater demand on an individual, for them to develop a life of prayer. Anyone that gives themselves over to the need and to the power of prayer, they don't have the time to mind the matters of everyone else.

I have come to know that God is more determined to get me to know about me!

You will never be able to grow in the Lord having your nose stuck up in other people's business all of the time. Trust me; I know of some people who are the exact same in their spiritual demeanor as they were when I first met them some Forty years ago!

There has been no spiritual maturity in their lives, which is obvious to everyone who knows them. Yet they have always been alike the teacher's pet in the classroom. They are always welcome to bring reports to the pastor on the other people.

Just to think of these types of people as being the better trusted individuals in the churches, is rather heartbreaking and thoroughly disappointing.

New converts to salvation, upon encountering these types of people in the churches, can be made to wonder if they will even have a chance with God in the judgment?

Oh yea, many people are walking around now concerned and stressed about certain people of the churches.

It is my intention to help you to understand why it is that the bible says to us that it better to trust in God than to put confidence in man. [Psalms 118:8-

9;]

God can be trusted because God is sure in every manner of His being. There is nothing at all questionable about God; the character of God is totally sound and accurate according to the written word of God.

It doesn't make sense, and certainly doesn't make faith to have any questions about the character of God!

Some people only come to the alter to approach the presence of God, curious just to see if God can do what they say that He can do?

Curiosity has driven them to be unsure as to whether God is even who He says that he is indeed!

These days, people are determined to charge God for the ill behavior of the people who claim to be saved. It is not the fault of God that people that confess to know Him; that they refuse to surrender their all to Him.

They don't even know Him at all in the pardoning of their sins, all becsuse of the curiosity in their heads.

The spirit of God changes people to measures so remarkable and wonderfully amazing, that they are hardly recognizable to those who knew them before the change.

Curiosity killed the ability to believe God, and it totally shuts off the reason ability to receive the Lord's prophets.

Curiosity seeks the Lord's stuff for personal possession and financial gain; faith seeks the Lord that we may be made the personal possession of the Lord's!

Eight

Incontinent Love

Love not the world, neither the things that are in the world. If any man love the world, the love of the Father is not in him. For all that is in the world, the lust of the flesh, and the lust of the eyes, and the pride of life, is not of the Father, but is of the world. 1 John 2:15-16;

Incontinent ~ Licentious, lustful, unchaste, uncontrolled, unrestrained. Having no or insufficient voluntary control, lacking self-control.

Incontinence has no intended purposeful destination. It's that spirit which motivates the wandering uninhibited release of movement or of motion.

It is actually most important to know where you are going in your life, when you are traveling to any destination, being cognizant when of whaterver it is that you are conveying to any listener to your conversation? Alike right now as you read this book you are aware that my intention is to appeal to the overwhelming since of curioisty, that may be festering inside of your brain.

In this life of which we have been given and blessed to live, we should be intent and purposeful of the direction of our destiny, rather than just to have the notion to realize that you are just actively in motion, moving in any direction, going onward to somewhere, but for unspecified reasons?

Knowing where we're going, when we are to arrive at our destinations and why we're on the move to get there initially, it gives the more assured expectation of what we are going there to receive, and and not just an ignighted assumption loaded with the hype enough to devastate you, when your expectation fails to deliver.

Of who it is, or may be on the other hand, that we may be going to be delivering the gift package of our love to it is much more reasonable to be stable and sound in our decisions to move progressively onward to share our love.

Love; demands an automated intellectual but also an actuated return right back to the giver who shared their love with us at first! The moment it is released and sent outwards to the objective person of its impelled destination, love expects a qualified response, compatible to its level of introspective plant.

Since Love believed;(I Corinthians 13:5-7) that any person would be worthy of being loved, one should also believe that the giver of the love is also worthy of being loved in response. Given Love, should never have been thought to have been given to anyone, but invain!

At all times, the intended destination of love can't be intermingled with the feelings of twisted emotions, and lustful desires of the flesh, being the ultimate motivations for the connectivity.

Love requires that we take out the time to examine the objects of our affections and our inner-selves. To assure ourselves that we are not getting into the most disastrous painful experiences of our lives, of which might have been thought to be love relationships?

Sure, purposeful, actual, temperate, hallowed love will be the reasons that we will have chosen to love the right persons and the integral amplitude of applied indulgence of one's self to love. So many people have either been instructed or habitually informed in the wrong idealisms of curious-centric ideas, concerning love.

The so-called definitive expressions of love are all over the place! As people are often so unstable in their thinking and their lifestyles. Many live and behave as though they have on and off switches installed in their hearts and minds, and definitely in their intellectual perceptions of living and of life altogether.

From God's perspective, which is the only perspective that really matters, Love is the greatest thing that we have in the entire cosmos! There is nothing at all greater than Love! The whole

world was created and fashioned according to the love of God. Love knows one direction, which is that of forwardly progressive giving!

While it is a reality that most people are looking for love in all of the wrong places, the truth is that retrospectively we are to be giving the love that everyone else is looking for. Should everyone indulge themselves in giving love, there could be no way that anyone on the face of this planet could ever be found in search of finding love! (Quote unquote)

The issues is that everything other than love have gotten hold of people now days. For every reason that we are able to think of and of all of the reasons that we could never fathom in our minds. Nowadays, more people are out of control! Willfully, a higher percentage of people have substituted insatiable lust over and against the discipline of love, refined.

Lust selfishly demands what it desires, while thinking not much at all about the contributor which fulfill the lustful desire. Lust leaves love out in the cold, unsatisfied! So much more is required to confront the demands for love, from both the giver and the receiver!

It is paramount to respect the examples of loving and of love perspectively. God; being Love, He started with Love, desiring love from His most Loved creation! This was so that we who are capable of loving in return could both see why it is that we should also love as God loved us, and to know the proper manner in which to both give and to receive Love.

That means that we should know how to be

lovers! Meaning, that we be adequately informed of God's love for us, so as to the true lovers of God; to love our parents and siblings, our families, our neighbors and our friends,etc.. It is extremely important to give love, to receive love, to walk in love, to love our fellowman, and to be representatives of the Love of God, to all mankind.

Pinpointed Accuracy of Love

My friends, love is the arrow which when released from the archer's bow, it hits the bullseye of the target every single time with pinpointed accuracy. Real true love will never miss it's target, as the insightful ability of love is more assured than to that of a laser beam. The power of love denies any such thing as, inaccuracy and or of a blinded failure to love!

There is actually no real such thing as trying to love someone, or an intention to love them! Either you do love them or you don't simply because you have refused to do so. Love is never make-believe or fictitious! Loving someone is the easiest thing to do! You can love them when you can't even live in the same house with them.

In many instances, I am led myself to believe that we watched way too many cartoons, comic shows, and entertainment television. The idealistic images of love were drawn and painted like the valentines heart shaped box of candy. We were always hearing of love, while hearing the adults talk about who was in love and about to be married.

The mistakes were made, in that the televisions programing were allowed to teach us it's ideas, theories and philosophies of love. We were lured into accepting love as being a thing of fluff and goose pimples. The ideas of love, caused us to embrace love as being giggles and grins, and goofy expressions on our faces as results of the embarrassment brought on to us when we felt the tug and the pull towards another individual.

We were so allowed to think of love in such a plastic and playful manner that we never took the time to be educated and informed of the differential aspects of the truth of what love is actually! And of course what real true love is not at all about.

Growing up in elementary and middle school, Valentine's Day was always regarded as a very exciting day, because of the purported love that it was to bring. We were allowed to pass out valentine's cards to each other in our classrooms. The response that we would receive had altering effects on most everyone for the rest of the school year almost.

While some were encouraged to care, others could have cared less, and the attitude of caring for others grew with each of us, at each passing day as we matured. We were more likely to leave all of the caring for the other students at the school, where it all came about. Looking back over it all now as an adult, I'm reminded of the calm that all of the love gifts brought about, all around the school.

The instruction to us all, for the love day was simply for us to be involved if we wanted to. Perhaps had there been pinpointed accurate teaching and instruction for love and for loving others, the world that we know of today would be a different world.

This being the reasons that many who have married their high school sweethearts, a vast majority of them would not have ended their marriages in divorce court? Perhaps many would have been able to graps and to live according to the scripture, the commitment of the marriage vows, to live together until' death would part them!

Here is what I am saying. School aged children were much too young and immature to know whether they were in love, seriously infatuated, or if they only had acid indigestion?(LOL) This is what most of the students were encouraged and allowed to take away on their journeys, for the rest of their lives! That is of course until they were better informed and had learned the truth about love.

People love and express what they feel is love on a daily basis, yet all of the while they are in question as to what love really is? A multiplicity of questions are plaguing the reason-ability in the minds of most people. People are not stable as to who, how, when, and of where it is that they are to show love, to give love, or even if to be in love?

For several decades now, the ideas of falling in love have taken on such a darken perspective, whereas many people believe that such love experiences are to be levied upon everyone and anything of their own emotional choosing.

The language description for the many things of which we may have become overwhelmed with, is now become something that we have labeled as being in love with it.

The greater truth is that people choose to allow

for their expressions of love to be realized all over the place. For many it can never be said definitively, whether they are lovers or haters!

Listening to the language of the conversations from some certain people, it could never be said that they are indeed haters, but it for sure that they can't be recognized as lovers, either.

Neutrality is the positions of feelings and emotional expressions, of which many of these latter generations are choosing to stand in. They have been led to believe that they are protecting themselves from being rejected, jilted, and or even painfully scarred. Likewise they are believing to have affixed themselves to remain single and free willed, having no responsible connections to give of themselves.

I find it difficult to understand how it is that people feel that they can just keep on giving, while simultaneously they have checked out on the possibilities of ever feeling anything at all. The accusations of being closed minded and not willing to accept the need for being changed are hurled in the direction of those who are direct and intentional of what love is and of where it is that they are sure that their love belongs.

More time is spent in the teaching environments of so many of the churches and other secular teaching institutions, instructing us of what we ought to indeed love or to be willing to love. There is more of a reality of truths relative to the things that we are not to love! There are many things that we simply ought to purposefully avoid, in an effort not to contaminate the love and or even the love desire that we all possess.

Far too often love is defined and taught to be viewed as unconditional acceptance. No matter what, when we are thought to be people of real love, it is often expected that we will be open to everything everywhere, from any people. There is more confusion than there could ever be of understanding and definitive reasoning to these types of teaching.

It is not beneficial at all to any of us, whenever we allow ourselves to love all of this and all of that as well, all at the same time! Incontinence is the culprit cause of bringing confusion to the hearts and the minds of the people everywhere! Love demands a decision to be made! Incontinent love is a real lie, let loose to roam free and wild, like wolves and the beast of in the forest!

It is so necessary to put and intentional difference between what it is that we love and what it is that we hate. Love and hate are as different and opposite as the sun and the moon, or rather as darkness and the light are totally different. There is no such thing as good bad, or bad good! It is either good or it is bad!

The watchful intentions of our expressions of love are to always be separated from all expressions of hatred, so as to prevent us from the twisted frequency to develop a love to hate, or an hatred for loving.

The things that we hate should never be in the forefront of our thinking. It is a truth that the things that we allow for ourselves to think on a consistent basis, that it shapes the development of what we eventually become.

As the lines between loving and hating have

been blurred. The minds of many so called free thinkers have run away all over their psycho analytical processes of thinking. They're on a mental roller coaster ride from hell, that will never let them get off of the journey of the ride, until the destructive end.

Unrestrained, Misguided, Unintentional Curiosity

Curiosity has got the world spinning and rolling in every direction but to the Lord! Many are feeling as if they are spinning like a tornado or a spinning top, while they are on a never ending merry-go-round. Others are now riding so high, they appear to posture themselves as if they are flying higher than the clouds in the sky.

Never the less, as their curiosity has taken over and have flooded and drowned their sober minds, they're all on a ride! Some are riding on unicycles, while some are on bicycles. Others are riding tricycles or three wheelers if you prefer, while others are riding all that are four wheelers of the speedier types.

I prefer the metaphorical aspect of riding to the likes of that of a roller coaster. As this metaphor is applied to this literary work, it is intended that you picture the roller coaster as our own human forms, curiously rolling out of control through the journey of life.

The ride is always up and down, fast and then slow. Jerking our necks as if to give us whiplash as the speed increases without even giving us a notice of the change in velocity and the steep curves along the railroad like journey.

Incontinent Love

The roller coaster is definitely curiously rolling out of control, never planning on rolling to where it was never intended to end up at the finish of the journey! The roller coaster is controlled by the track that it runs on. The tracks directs the roller coaster on the journey having the roller coaster fastened to the tracks.

Usually, the tracks have built in breaking systems installed to manage and to control the limit of the speed as it rolls around the track.

Alike most curious people, their minds are made up that they are not following any rules, and no one will ever tell them what to do and how to live their lives. Without realizing it they are derailed and often off of the track.

They may see where they are, but they cannot find a since of appreciation for being so curious about being at another place in their lives. Being self centered and always self willed, it's been easy to be swayed to take a look and a possible leap into the very next presentation of curious attractions.

The ride was curiously driven to see just where it could possibly arrive as result of creating it's own destination, if it just went about it's own way! There was absolutely no considerations taken for the assessment of the journey. Not prepared for disregarding the regulatory standard requirements for traveling beyond the borders into unknown territories.

Nothing has been really regarded as necessary for journeying as a nomad or a vagabond, of which they who are on the curious journey are unintentionally more destined to become. They are moving in any direction having no methods of replenishing their supply when it will have all been exhausted.

From the beginning of it's initial release, it's been determined never to follow the mapped out journey of the track. Somehow it has decided on making up it's own journey, for the ride? The conductor for the ride has been thrown overboard! Voices of reason and instructions have been silenced, and shut down.

Directions and instructions have been cited as binding and imprisoning for a free traveler. Doesn't matter that just up the way another free traveler has been derailed and had been thrown off of the track. Some way or another they are convinced that it won't happen to them.

But just as it seemed that they were getting on with their own plans to move ahead and to live at their own pace, something or someone broadsides them, causing them to collide with a disaster.

In this instance, from the start, I need for you to see yourselves as the roller coaster, not just as the riders on the expedition for a since of recreation. You're the one responsible for the journey that you're driving on! We all must be on the guided tour, as instructed by the tour guide.

Roller coasters pick up speed as they decline the highs after what seemed to be a long but steep up hill climb! They always appear to slow down on their way up, but they increase in momentum as they begin to approach the lows of the ride.

Literally, the amusement park roller coaster is moving at a rate too high in speed for picking up other passengers as they travel the concourse.

Incontinent Love

Figuratively speaking, the differences are that we get high jacked while on our own rebellious journeys, as result of failing to avoid certain paths of danger and of in-assurance.

As the track of which the roller coaster rides on, has twists and turns for the sake of entertainment and excitement, it has never been the plans nor the desires of the rides inventors for the roller coaster to have been multi-directional in its travel for the journey. It would then end up being a journey ending ride of disaster!

The roller coaster moves in one direction, which is often either forwards or sometimes backwards, through the journey, from the star to the finished end of the ride. Doesn't matter how pleasant the ride just might be to the rider, the ride must be enjoyed in one direction at a time, even though curiosity would prefer to turn the one directional ride into a multi-directional spin of an event.

I have not been the witness of seeing a roller coaster change directions in the middle of the ride, while never stopping to change the direction. Once the momentum causes us to speed up in our travels, life dictates that our forward progress must be brought to a complete halt if we desire to change direction.

Should the directions change, it has been my experience that the ride is being redirected to return to the starting point. It have never been sent into a direction which leaves the park! The ride never takes its passengers hostage, taking them away from the intended recreational experience.

No matter how we choose to roll in this life, someone else will desire to roll with us. Our since of responsibility will always caution us to pay attention to our behavior and or the manner of which we conduct ourselves, knowing that someone else's life may be in our hands?

Some people are yet in a since of disbelief that they had been responsible for shattering the lives of someone else who had chosen to ride with them. They were insensitive to the desires of the other's cries, as their curiosity had been satisfied beyond the limit, and they now wanted to go back to where they all started. They didn't want to go any further!

The roller coaster had strayed too far in the wrong direction and couldn't find it's way back. Alike a launched rocket into outer space, it loses parts of it's original mechanical makeup. Things automatically fall off and permanently dislodge themselves from the rocket, the further away that it gets from the launching pad.

An uncontrolled return to the start is never going to be the same as a controlled departure from the start. The manner in which you depart is going to be a determinate factor of the condition that you just may be in whenever you return. Be wise not to put yourselves in the position of needing much healing and deliverance at the point of your return.

Incontinent love is going to cause you to be in situations of incurable pains and disasters, which there may be no found cure or remedy. It is not at all wise to place your own selves in positions that you will eventually have to face having no explanations for how you ended up where you are. For sure, you will have no one else to blame for your destructive behavior, be yourself.

You Never Avoided It, Now You Love It!

THERE IS A WAY WHICH SEEMETH RIGHT UNTO A MAN, BUT THE END THEREOF ARE THE WAYS OF DEATH. PROVERBS 14:12;

It is not often possible to return on your own, to successfully rest at the starting point where you might have begun your journey, at will having had a change of mind, while likewise willfully following your own curiosity.

Because of your own indecisiveness, haven switched the desired directions in the middle of the track, your direction of travel is no longer intriguing, nor leading to the exact destiny of your intended destination.

Curiosity has left many people believing that life is all fluff, games and good times. They prefer to think that life ain't nothing but a party. The saddest thing about it is that many people live as though there is nothing else to do, but to party. It is paramount, that we always know our way back to the exact place where we started. This is the only way to ensure that we never be lost.

Life's cycles, of the reoccurring pleasures in all the world, will blind you at every turn in the curves that are thrust in the way as you journey. Imbalanced voids, of timeless curious explorations, while ignoring the warning signs and the fading light in the distances, are associative to trusting unto the actual deception of time, that can cause you to lose your life and even to lose your soul.

Time does have the powerful ability to bring about unwanted, unsuspected, inexplicable changes that one could have never been prepared for! In the wrong settings of the world, we will always find that the wrong things of destruction and death are moving with the cadence in the rhythm of time, on the hunt for the most unsuspecting victims!

Falling in love with the pleasures of life can often set us up unintentionally to avoid the necessity to be watchful of time. In our youth, many of us had parents that might just warm out backsides, whenever we allowed for the time to run away, while we were out with friends having what we thought of as a good time.

Many of those times might have been wiled away getting involved with being encouraged to try things that we never had even thought of doing before. Someone else always desire to do the things that you will have intentionally avoided! The thing that we will have purposefully chosen never to do, even at the instruction of our parents, others might have never learned or desired to obey.

We simply don't have forever and all of the time in the world to make the right choices and the right decisions. Time moves on forward faster than every distracted mind could ever realize. By the time that we will have come to ourselves, we will have to realize that we had outright fallen in love, with the misbehavior of the misguided experiences.

The word of God admonishes us to avoid loving the world and the things of the world. Those who lean more to their own curiosity, they need more explanations, and need to be given reasonable instruction which appeal to their own thinking.

It is not until they had discovered that they had fallen and they can't get up, as result of thrusting themselves downward into the pleasures of the world, that they even consider the word of the scripture. Most people often believe that they are in total control of things, until it had been revealed to them that they had their hands on the wrong knobs all along. They never knew where they were headed from the beginning.

They had fallen in love with the fact that they were indeed moving forward according to their own desired will. So they never paid much attention to the weary winding road and that it was leading to an unsuspected end, right over the edge of the cliff! Their own selfish lustful ride, would lead them to a dreadful untimely death!

Figuratively speaking, this metaphorical grasp was written to show just how easy it has been to lose control, and to end up at an end, which had been thought to be the beginning of the best good time that any person could ever have. Many met the fate of their doom as their ride plunged them over the edge downwards into the depths of death and destruction.

Somehow, others were met with grace and the mercy of God, being blessed to escape death! They were given another chance to live! Don't take the chance of being as blessed as the other persons were that escaped. Get a grip, and settle yourselves to seek God;s guidance through the written word of God.

Apply the time to learn to follow after the ways of God's examples of Love. Curiosity has the ability to mask the hatred just tucked away underneath incontinent love!

Now the choice is yours; right or wrong! Good or bad; You Choose!

Nine

"Prohibition ~ Free Living" "[Anything Goes]"

Only be thou strong and very courageous, that thou mayest observe to do according to all the law, which Moses my servant commanded thee: turn not from it to the right hand or to the left, that mayest prosper withersoever thou goest. This book of the law shall not depart out of thy mouth; but thou shall meditate therein day and night, that thou mayest observe to do according to all that is written therein: for then thou shalt make thy way prosperous, and then thou shalt have good success.   Joshua 1:7-8

> BLESSED IS THE MAN THAT WALKETH NOT IN THE COUNSEL OF THE UNGODLY, NOT STANDETH IN THE WAY OF SINNERS, NOR SITTETH IN THE SEAT OF THE SCORNFUL. PSALMS 1:1
>
> AND EVEN AS THEY DID NOT LIKE TO RETAIN GOD IN THEIR KNOWLEDGE, GOD GAVE THEM OVER TO A REPROBATE MIND, TO DO THOSE THINGS WHICH ARE NOT CONVENIENT; BEING FILLED WITH ALL UNRIGHTEOUSNESS, FORNICATION, WICKEDNESS, COVETOUSNESS, MALICIOUSNESS, FULL OF ENVY, MURDER, DEBATE, DECEIT, MALIGNITY, WHISPERERS, BACKBITERS, HATER OF GOD, DESPITEFUL, PROUD, BOASTERS, INVENTORS OF EVIL THINGS, DISOBEDIENT TO PARENTS, WITHOUT UNDERSTANDING, COVENANT BREAKERS, WITHOUT NATURAL AFFECTION, IMPLACABLE, UNMERCIFUL: WHO KNOWING THE JUDGMENT OF GOD, THAT THEY WHICH COMMIT SUCH THINGS ARE WORTHY OF DEATH, NOT ONLY DO THE SAME, BUT HAVE PLEASURE IN THEM THAT DO THEM. ROMANS 1:28-32

Curiosity enabled Lifestyles; have no rules.

The American society in which we now live has been chocked full of people who have determined that life should be lived as free as every individual desires for it to be lived, having absolutely no prohibitions of any kind.

However it's an idea that is not at all brand new to the human idealism of living. And existing as the dominating species of all earthly living beings on the face of this planet.

Although many of the beast of the animal kingdom can tear us to shreds as a result of their powerful brute strength and instinct to kill and to devour prey. We are more powerful than they are from the standpoint of out innate intelligibility to entrap them.

Being more intelligent to reasonably out think

them, and to dominate using their fierce natural desires to kill, against them.

While they think that they are about to have us as their prey, we are thinking swiftly on our feet on how to lure them, to come in just a bit closer to us, so that we can have them in a net or a cage of some sort. We can often have the animals when they could never have us as their prey.

The bible instructs us in the knowledge of the fact that it was Adam indeed who named all of the animals of the earth. Using the authority given to him from the creator of the earth and all of the life forms in the earth.

The God-Head counseled Himself; deciding to speak to the created man in the earth telling him the rules and regulations of the garden. Forbidding him from doing certain things such as eating and touching the fruit of the forbidden trees in the midst of the garden.

Remember that it was indeed God's idea that mankind should have the rule and domination in the earth. But, God did so knowing that we as man could never be successful in the earth outside of being ruled and governed. The brilliance of the human mind being more vastly expansive to imagine and to reason, could not be left to itself alone to rule in the earth.

God created human beings knowing that we would need firstly to obey the laws and to follow the rules before we would ever truly be the custodial ruler-ship in the earth to enforce and to encourage other men of the earth to also follow the rules and or to obey the laws of the land.

All over the face of the planet, it is a common

thing to hear people say that they do not choose to believe the bible or the bible teachings, all because of the rules and the governing of the scripture.

People want to do exactly what they want to do, and that is exactly what they do on a daily basis! Doesn't seem to matter to them of the consequences for the choices of their behavior! They are determined to do just as they are pleased to do so, because it's what they want to do, no matter of what anyone else thinks.

People appear to be no longer aware of the dangers of choosing to defy the authority of the scriptures. God won't be arguing with mankind over the authority of the established scriptures. The written word of God had already been settled in heaven forever.

A very common misnomer and even a serious determination among judicial authority, is to deputize other men to enforce the law today. The unlawful people are often the ones employed to do so; being cited as criminally brilliant. They had been known to slip through the cracks of the law undetected, even though, albeit, they got caught!

I learned early on in the church, that the law, is for the lawless! Our society has been gravely unsuccessful at enforcing the law, simply for the true lack of convictions, as it relates to the given laws. Simply because of people who have outright chosen to disregard and to intentionally disobey the laws, and the law enforcement officers of the law.

Also note; that many of the people of today's society have major problems with showing respect for the law enforcement officers. Consistently there are rifts and uproars among the citizens and the local police of almost every major city in the USA!

It is often that those who are indeed lawless, they think that they have found the need to instruct the law enforcement officers of the laws of the land. People who don't follow the law by design; they think that they have the right to hold law enforcement officials to a standard that they even themselves totally despise!

Many of the people who have made a life of crime, breaking the laws of the land intentionally, they feel as if they should be allowed to continue onward in their lifestyle without penalties or restrictions to their own choices of behavior.

To the lawless; it makes all kinds of sense to them to just live and let live? I sort believe that their motto ought to be; "just don't bother." When truly pressed to give an account for their behavior as a criminal, they just may be quick to acknowledge that everybody is doing the same things, as they are, themselves!

Even when you know for a fact firsthand that others are in need of counsel and or of swiftly being checked for their behavior, the admonishment to you is don't tell it! The rules for the lawless among the society; and nowadays even among the rebels in the churches is that "snitches get stitches!"

Just keep it to you and let things work itself out over time, all on its own. Many leaders of the churches are now suggesting that nobody need for anyone else, to be telling them what to do and how to live their own lives.

We are actually living in a day and time that people are now more-so comfortable having confessing, presently active sinners in the pulpit. Preaching to other unsaved sinners about salvation! And deliverance to free them from penalties and the bondage of sin.

The more popular choices for the people of the churches are that they want leadership that keep it real! When it get to be real messy and really ungodly up in the sanctuary of the churches, those same members of the said churches who never preferred truly saved and delivered leaders, are attempting to cry foul now since things are indeed messed up!

Somehow, many of the people of the churches are deceived in that they have decided against hearing from those persons who confess to have been washed in the blood of the Lamb of God; and filled with the Holy Ghost! Having non-contradicting lifestyles for living their lives daily.

They need to have people who wear the scars of a presently sinful lifestyle; and who bear the scent of the stench of hell's fragrance all over their person, to lead them in the way of the church.

Likewise, the people in the pews who are aware of the ungodly behavior and the lack of convictions of the leaders that they have chosen to lead them, are also the ones who feel that they have a word for the preachers, and or for the leadership in the churches.

People now want leaders that they themselves can lead and instruct and guide through their tinier as the leader. They like following a leader in whom they say of themselves; "they can't tell me anything; I know all of their secrets and their junk!"

People have setup a resistance for prohibition even before they have an understanding of the true purpose and knowing how it is that they will benefit as a citizen of the kingdom of God; the community.

And, even the state in which they are living, being and obedient observer of the laws. Code-compliance officers of the city can often be a disruption to daily living for those whose properties are out of compliance to the city and or of the state's ordinances. Whether they like it or not, they have to come up to code!

Believe me, no being is greater than that of mankind; although the beast of the field and many of the fishes in the ocean and the sea are greater in size and brutally increased in strength! Many animals of the wild can take out a human being with one swipe of their paw; clawing us to death suddenly.

The written accounts in the bible are psychologically bewildering to many people who look into the word of God; but from a very unbelieving faithless humanistic perspective. Just how it is that we could be made in the image and in the likeness of God sounds so farfetched to the natural human mind; as such thinking is so farther expanded, much more than the scientific minds of the curious theorist, and explorers of our human involvement in the earth.

Ever since the foul infraction in the Garden of Eden; mankind have been on a quest of acquiring more knowledge. Even though it has been

proven that we as mankind have learned certain things and are assured that we have the understanding of the knowledge of the things that we have learned, the curious mind still wonders if there is still more to know about that to which we have indeed come to know; never satisfied.

I have personally come to know people who have proven that they have indeed outsmarted themselves, with all of the knowledge to which they had acquired. Growing up I used to hear the terminology often used which stated that you can be too smart for your own good? Of course we have seen whereas certain people had drummed up what would be later termed as brilliant criminal schemes.

However those people discovered that law enforcement had also been drumming up schematic methodology to catch the criminally astute in the midst of their criminal scheme; and to their surprise they did get caught! I am driving to the point in fact that people do know the rules for living and they are also aware of the laws of the land, only they choose to ignore the knowledge that they have already on the inside of their heads.

Many people are even very knowledgeable of the scripture from the standpoint of their head knowledge; they have no life of knowledge of the word in their heart! Nothing on the inside of them causes them to respect the word of God whereas they apply the word knowledge to their scheme and their standard of living. They fight vigorously with everything on the inside of themselves to disregard the messages of the Holy Writ of God.

The more time that I have spent getting to know new people whether they be people of the neighborhood, the church, co-workers, and of course just simply when bumping into people while running errands or sitting in a restaurant; not much time is spent in a conversation when people will begin to reveal their disdain for following any rules, in one way or another. They just believe that anyone who comes into contact with them ought to know exactly how they feel about the establishment of rules, and of laws which are designed to govern their behavior of living.

Curiosity gets people stirred up right down in the middle of their gutter-most being, whereas they want to do what everybody else does; they want to have what everybody else has; they want to go where everybody else is going, and so forth? People are willing to walk through the fire sometimes literally just for the sake of satisfying their curiosity at all and at any cost?

Many of our brothers and sisters who are living on the streets homeless without the shelter of having their place of residence; they have landed themselves in those living conditions due to the fact that they would neither respect nor obey the rules and the laws of the land of which they live. Some people refuse to pay a bill just to see how long they can continue to enjoy the benefit without being interrupted.

It blows my mind to see so many people who are angered and totally put out with God, because things went array for them when in fact they knew what the word of God says about living, but they chose to live contrary to the word and to the will

of God for their lives. They have turned it around in their heads that God ought to be pleased with the way that they live regardless! They have overlooked the fact that they need to please the Lord; living according to the word of God.

Prohibition-Free living doesn't suggest that you are free indeed to live as you choose; but, it does suggest that you need to feel free to do and to try whatever your heart and your mind tells you? This is the reason that the statements are so frequently verbalized that no one can judge me but God; God knows my heart; if God didn't want me to try it, He would have never put it here in the earth; and so on?

Many of these so-called people are given the titles of being free-spirited people. These same people most of them have tried and have done so many prohibited things right down to the bottom of their early graves; many of them even knew the outcomes and the final destinations of their own fatal choices, but they chose to do them anyway!

Prohibition Free living, assures that you will never grow up and mature to be the responsible adult that you were designed to be as you are giving the privilege to grow in age and in respect of knowledge. Both aging and the acquisition of knowledge should have the effect on you as a person to aid you in realizing that certain things that you will have done while growing up are not to be repeated or chosen as a manner of living as an adult.

Doing the things that we know and are aware of the fact that they are indeed wrong should not be heralded as the given respectful right of your own free will to choose to do whatever you want to do; let it be acknowledged that it is indeed however your free will choosing to act out in sin! Especially since you know before you carry out the act of wrong doing, that it is indeed wrong before you do it; it is blatant sinful transgression of the word and the law of God.

I am aware that this is the reason that so many people refuse to go to church; they simply do not want to be told that they are wrong, or that God disapproves of their style of living. They just want to be left alone to live as they have chosen to do so; they are not going to be held accountable to the Holy Scripture! Many people will boldly say nowadays, "Well I know that it's wrong in your eyes, but not in my eyes; I make my own choices and my own decisions! Leave me alone; even if I do fall I want to be responsible for my own failure, not you or anyone else."

"It's My Life; So Just Let Me Live It!"

Prohibitions are boundaries set in place for specific reasons that are designed to protect and to secure us. We are to be secured, while we are living, not that we would ever need any such securities while our dead bodies lie in a grave.

There are so many reasons that you just can't make everybody your friends. You will often find, that there are some people who are driven absolutely bonkers! They literally fall apart at the seams over the reality of your ability to respect and to obey the set boundaries that you have installed for living your own life obeying the laws of the land. Some people will even suggest that you

need to relax. Go ahead and live a little; they say!

They want to know that you are just as dangerously wild, and as reckless in your decision making, as they are themselves. They may even ask if you ever get tired of doing what everybody wants you to do? Meaning following the laws and having respect for authority. We sort of like to refer to them as people who a living totally out of control!

My parents rules were that we were not free to go wherever we wanted to roam! For as long as we lived under their roof, without a second thought about it, we were going be asking their permission firstly! I would always seem to meet someone at school or out in the park playing ball or even at the church, who wanted me to go places without asking permission. I knew already that I was supposed to ask for permission, even though at times I might have gone along.

Curiosity, invites foolishness into the heart of teenagers and young people. Which they will all live to regret making the bad decisions which also led to the record of their past bad behavior. However, for some it is the cause of their present outlandish behavior. Of course that is if by the grace of God, they are allowed to continue living on to mature beyond the reckless behavior of self destructive, decision making.

Many parents are determined to raise their children as free spirits. They want them to experience life in any way that they choose to do so! They don't want for them to know of any prohibitions or boundaries. Every bad decision that the children make, the parents are right there on the spot to absorb the pain of their guilt, to make since of their child's sinceless behavior.

They feel that after being responsible for haven raised their child to do whatever their heart desired, they can explain the heart and the mindset of their child. This is most often seen whenever the child has been convicted for a crime, whereas they are now facing being sent to do time in prison.

Curiously, as a child is being allowed to raise themselves, they are not aware that their art of rebellious choosing and stubborn behavior, that it is growing up with them! But it is also growing beyond their own ability to control the outcomes, or even to set any boundaries. The day of reckoning always comes around sooner that one will have expected.

While most of us were raised to know what is indeed right from wrong, others were allowed to disregard wrong, and to shun the requirements for doing things right! Many of today's most notorious criminals are the same person's who were raised to do whatever they wanted to do, without being disciplined.

Whenever they see something that they want, there are no prohibitions regarded to deter them from going after the determination to to take it. Their curiosity has been found to be more powerful than the boundaries of the established laws of the land.

Others have grown up to be the very same convicted suspects who took the lives of their own parents or guardians. To often the rest of the people in the world are left to wonder and to ask the questions, why? They lack discipline and respect for authority! They have been raised to disallow anyone to tell them what to do or how to live their lives.

I attended school with some classmates who stayed in trouble consistently. They were determined to disrespect all boundaries, including all student and the faculty. They fought many of the other students and bullied different ones who were inferior to their attitude and behavior.

They would even attempt to fight physically with the adult teachers and staff. When the police were called, many of them had the mindset to resist being arrested. They never believed that they had done anything wrong enough to require the police being called on them.

Many others would have already done their damage and had fled the scene before having to face the authorities for their unacceptable behavior. They knew that they had done the wrong thing, they were just not going to answer to any disciplining authority.

Many, could be very sweet and loving young people, had they been disciplined to learn respect for others and for themselves. They have continued to live on as older individuals, only to wreck their own lives, through their learned behavior as a spoiled brat. They had convinced themselves to believe and to expect that everybody else would accept and give way to their stubborn refusal to obey and to follow the rules.

They Are Truly Monsters Now

Little monsters that are allowed to grow up as

unruly and just as contentiously disruptive as they can be, soon develop into grown up, bigger, uglier, more dangerous monsters, unable to mature into respectful adults! Even though they make attempts to do better, and or to better themselves, they will have already shut out the possibilities to genuinely absorb the lessons of living to transform their minds to think of changing.

Whereas, trouble used to come to them when they never intended or expected for it to, they often found themselves having to explain why it is that they had happened to be in the troubled situation they were in? As the monstrous adults they've become, they are now more apt to bring the trouble to any situation to which they are in, but shamelessly intentional!

Their mindsets are found never to be geared towards doing things that are right and respectful! They could careless about what anyone thinks of them! They have desensitized their hearts and their minds to reflect the criticism of everyone that disapproves of their behavior. You are going to find that they are not very cognizant of the consequences of any of their actions and decisions.

It could almost appear that they have seared off the ends of their own feelings and emotions. As they have practiced being cold in their responses, and totally shut off to the expectations of showing remorse.

A young teenager shot and killed a police officer. When he was discovered to be attempting to steal a car, he panicked in fear and reached for a gun that he was carrying and pulled the trigger killing the officer. He just knew that he could lie his way out of doing what he did? Too many witnesses and the truth caused him to suffer the consequences for his actions. As a result, he was given life in prison without parole.

The young misbehaving children were often shunned and rejected because of their refusal to obey and to have respect for authority. As result of this type of reality in their lives, they learned to develop a since of callousness to make them rough on the exterior and in the interior of their emotions on the inside as well! They determined within themselves not to ever feel anything, if possible.

Being alone from our childhood up unto our adulthood, has always had a way of causing us to look in the mirror at our selves, to see our ways. As we became shameful of being dis-behaved, something would make us fear the unknown, just lurking about us in the room. We all knew to expect the discipline for our bad behavior, even though it never came for so many.

Automatically, we were afraid that the devil or being discovered for our wrong doing, was going to get us and take us away from our parents and our family's. It was as if we were made to feel that another presence had entered into the room with us?

Curiosity kicks in even when we are doing wrong, and may feel that we had gotten away with it. We find ourselves wondering if someone else had seen what we had done, or if they knew for sure that we were the guilty party?

We knew that it wasn't a good presence or even

a pleasant spirit looking over our shoulders! Was it just our conscience troubling us, or had it been that a real monster had come to check us for being in the darkness of our behavior?

Little children have often been afraid to sleep in their rooms by themselves, for fear of there being a monster under the bed, or hiding in the closet ready to come and to pounce upon them in the night. Especially after being bad!

When being reared to do your own thing and to respond or not, depending on how you may be feeling at the time, to the criticism of your behavior, the greater chances are that you were never taught to apologize and to say "I'm Sorry!" You were even allowed to think of things as being everybody else's fault that they happened the way that they did!

Living and doing things in your own ways, often causes others to be scarred and or permanently damaged in the destruction of your path. Other people's lives are always going to be effected in one way or another, whether the results be positive or negative.

We say that it is never too late to learn. But you have got to be able to desire changing for the sake of yourselves and for others.

It is quite senseless to me to allow for children who are fearful of monsters, to grow to become the monsters they all once feared!

Only these monsters are real human beings and they are never imaginary images hiding under the bed or in the closet. Even though they have not been able to physically touch or to visually encapsulate the images of the monsters they

feared, they were always convinced that they were indeed there!

Not having had the parental authority, as the parents refused to correct their behavior, or to direct them in the ways of future citizens of society, having respectful behavior to do what was right, no one was there to show them what just might become of them should they continue to live in the way of rebellion, and stubborn refusal to conform as they were required. The same as all people of the society are required to behave and to live.

They were not reared to continuously self-check themselves, so as to realize or to recognize the monstrous individuals they have now become. They refuse to embrace the fact that they have become their own horror show, in the flesh!

The monsters they once feared as a child are now hidden in the corners of the hiding places in their heads, tucked away in their attitudes, while blinding their minds. They can neither see or feel the danger that they now pose to society and definitely to themselves.

What is the most detrimental is that fact that they never intend to change living and behaving as they do. We are living witnesses to the realistic fact as a result of seeing and even watching certain people, that going to church alone does not cure the conditions of such persons.

It takes the power of God! One has to surrender to the word of God to accept the sacrifice of Jesus Christ, for His sacrifice of shedding His blood for all humanity on the cross at Calvary. You must believe that He was raised from the grave on the third day, with all power and authority in His hands.

The account of Jesus Christ is not a myth, or a fairytale, or a joke of any kind! You have got to ask Jesus to help you to change your ways, as your mind is also changes. He's the only one to reach into the heart and into the minds of any individual.

Jesus has all power over all sin, and unrighteousness. He can and He will do it for you, if you will allow for Him to! The time that you have spent being the unrestricted person that you are, doesn't prevent you from coming to the Lord, when the Lord indeed is drawing you to come to Him.

The Father in Heaven, knows who you are, He's worthy to draw you. If He draw you to come to Jesus, you can then come. However if He is not drawing you to come to Christ Jesus, perhaps your destiny may be chained and padlocked for eternal destruction!

Conclusion

"Take Hold Of Your Mind!"

> EVER LEARNING, NEVER ABLE TO COME
> TO THE KNOWLEDGE OF THE TRUTH.
> II TIMOTHY 3:7

His Name Is Perplexity ~ His Destiny Is Confusion
THE MONSTER

Those of which have acquired great influence and social authority, have done so as result of having absolutely no fear for diving in to see for themselves! While disregarding prohibitions of any kind. They are the voices that many will prefer to listen to, willing to apply the information given to them.

Many have amassed great financial wealth, having reached up into the more recognized realms of higher education. Whether they really know or not, because of the acknowledged levels of graduate degrees behind their names, they are automatically accepted to be in the know about most anything.

What will not be readily available to see of those preferred individuals are often the whirlwind of star wars and galactic battles, swirling around in their brains. They are often labeled as mentally fractured, or out right crazy. Usually, informatively, they are too much for the average person. Their knowledgebase have been broadened, even too much for themselves.

They have often explored into the forbidden, unknown realms, so far out away from grounded psychological realms of the head room of their minds, seeking to know that which has never been awarded for the minds of humanity.

For this reason alone, they have convinced themselves that they are smarter than the average human being. We often think of them as being rather kooky!

At will, by their own choices back at the beginning of their youth, they entered into the world of perplexity, on the vehicles of perpetual inquisitions of everything! Their parents or guardians have often failed to pay attention to the fact that they lacked comprehensive understanding, failing to ever learn. They have been allowed to venture out as far as they liked.

While they never did grasp onto the necessary things of knowledge and the general aspects of growing as a child, they were allowed to wander into all of the realms of fiction and make believe imagination and the cartoon psi-fi stories that lead them astray for the foundational platforms of growth.

It is very easy to think that what we are witnessing are the levels of success to which such inquisitive people have secured. With that, of course, being the ultimate levels that other perplexed people believe that they are seeking to achieve.

The higher up, and the longer that they travel on that road of perplexity, they actually become perplexed as a way of envisioning the world of which they live.

Perplexity, is the breeding grounds, whereas questions have but only the ability to produce other questions, and more perplexing questions to be exact! Nothing is ever believed to be clearly understood or comprehended as the correct answer. Nothing is ever absolute!

Perplexity alleviates the basis for which we are to believe in our sober minds that the ground which we are seeking to build our own lives upon, that it is ever going to be solid enough to build an acceptable foundation for the desired house of our dreams.

While they remain perplexed, they are eventually destined to arrive as a certified citizen, in the city of confusion! People that are truthfully confused, they are of the very last people to believe that they are confused. They are going on about their lives thinking that most everyone else that they come into contact with, they are confused and twisted themselves!

Others may not have successfully matriculated to mature sinking into their perplexity, whereas they are finally confirmed as being mentally and psychologically unfit for the society. They are still examining their own inability to grasp and to hold onto what has been established as the truth.

They celebrate their ability to deny facts, continuing to dig beneath the bottom, where there is really nothing else to locate there, according to what they are indeed looking for. Or even to find!

Speaking with many really educated people, so called; you are soon able to understand why it has been established that they had spent the balance of their adult life in higher learning institutions.

They're pregnant with questions that crash and destroy the scales that should establish that their mental balance has been completely aligned to live in the established truth of God's word!

Only, at the time of birthing the answers, to questions and receiving acceptable solutions to problems, their intellectual womb has been set to the tune of rejection!

Automatically, the mental womb resends the inquiry back into fetal developmental stage to begin the process of search and find all over again. What should be the very beginning of growing and the true process of growth, has become perpetually the beginning stages of asking questions, that are to forever be unanswered, as result of being denied .

The motivational issues which drove me to write

this literary work should be very clear to every reader of this book, at this point. It had been hinged on multiple factors, relative to the hindering inability blanketing the head space of the mental capacity, of those who's curiosity has been in overdrive.

The realization in the minds of those who were at once individual liberalizers of thought, since the time of their own deliverance, they now recognize the need for identifying the causes behind the faithlessness of many people in the churches nowadays, . Why it is they didn't, or couldn't get it!

Even many who are already labeled as consistent church attending believers, they are they which had also been attending the churches as confessing members, who claim to be convinced of the message of the gospel of the death, burial, and the resurrection of Jesus Christ. Even though the gospel has been held in Cue. They can't be sure that they accept and believe that the gospel is even truth!

These are the very same people that do the same things consistently in the churches since their childhood. They had been taught to attend Sunday School, and the other training sessions of the churches. For which the teaching nor the teachers had ever held their attention enough to release the door of their hearts, to allow the truth to enter in.

Something other than the teachings of the churches always seemed to intrigue their curiosity to see what was outside of the church, in the worldly society. While a certain percentage

of the churches youth were in attendance, others, whose parents were curious of the offerings of the secular influence, placed them in other activities not always in the proximity of the churches.

During the summer vacation, most of the churches would also sponsor a Summer Vacation Bible School. For which even the youth of the community were encouraged to attend. By the way of public schooling and of course private schooling also, it may have been better suggested that they attend other educational programs, and scouting for both boys and girls.

The boys and the girls attended sporting camps to further prepare them for being better enabled to compete for the next fiscal year of school sports. The teachers and the instructors as well as the other adults that were in charge, took it upon themselves to introduce to the young people in attendance, to all sorts of idealisms and belief systems. Comparing them to that of the teachings of the bible and of course Christianity.

While the direct intention for the other ideas to be compared to that of the churches activities, they were determined to give them something other to do than what they had been taught in the churches. The secular teachers and instructors thought it might be beneficial if they supplied another avenue for the younger people to explore.

As I have grown as an adult and matured as a responsible parent and as a leader of the churches, I have taken advantage of the opportunities to teach the younger people of the teachings to watch out for and even to avoid. Younger immature minds are incapable of deciphering when that which seems to good to be true, that it is indeed not good for them at all!

It is so important for them to know that many things that may be taught to them have very subtle and deceptive messages that will cause them to choose a life of making some very destructive choices in their lives.

Too often, the messages underneath the immediate extreme sensational good feelings, have led to many disturbing realities revealing just how bad the decisions were!

At such young and tender ages they were also being taught that there was no time for studies of faith in God, of which included the mandates for proper living in the bible. I can remember it being told to the whole group of those of us who were attending summer band camps, and football, basketball, baseball, Marshall arts summer league practices, to leave all of that God stuff at the church!

Sadly though, in many of the churches, the people are being led to believe that curiosity may eventually lead a pathway to acquiring faith. Many diverse things will happen in the lives of all people, but the meaningful messages gleaned, only yield the actual lessons through the written word of God.

How to feel and what to do about the feelings that we might have garnered, need much instruction to inform us of whether it can produce faith, or destroy faith in God. Curiosity have the dependence upon what may commonly occur in the lives of other people. However, to rely upon the word of God can show us whether or not to take in the lessons, or to discard them totally.

My advice to you is that you never allow for yourselves to carried away with being curious. Only the word of God; and God is the truth! It is accurately reliable for living by faith in God. If whenever you desire to acquire faith in God, you have got to turn to God through the written word!

Sin and iniquity, having been committed as a result of your curiosity, can never excuse you of the sinful offense committed. Repentance is still very much necessary for being cleansed and washed in the precious blood of Jesus Christ. Those who either fail or refuse to repent, they will suffer the penalty of eternal destruction!

Even those who commit crimes on the basis of their curiosity, being curiously motivated to commit the crime does not lend to the burden of proof to a judge or a jury enough to acquit the guilty party of the offense committed.

> For God is not the author of confusion, but of peace, as in all churches of the saints.
> 1 Corinthians 14:33

God will never confuse anybody! See that monster curiosity among us, is now identified as being called confusion! There is never anything good or positive that comes from confusion, disaster, trouble and destruction. However there is a remedy for the plight of being confused, for those who move quickly to dispel the actuality.

The gripping hold of confusion can be broken and destroyed through the powerfully shed blood of Jesus Christ. Permanently displacing the curious cause from your lives. The power of the blood can scrub every corner of your curiously confused mind if you will allow the Lord to do so.

The indwelling power of the Holy Ghost will keep your minds at peace, for ever. Nothing can ever happen in your lives that could ever block or bind the moving spirit of the Holy Ghost to keep Him from freeing you from falling into the depths of depression, or from being stressed out, and to comfort and to keep you safe in His arms!

Accept the Love that God has for you, then you will realize that you are too blessed to be stressed! I wrote a song titled; "Keep My Mind Lord." Science has deceptively cause people to believe that they are in total control of all of their thinking capacity. It's just that the masked destruction tuck away underneath the data, which came in with curiosity, is subtly set to go off and to explode right in the middle of your minds. Get Free and Have Peace!